How To...

GET GREAT GUITAR TONES

The Ins and Outs of Various Guitars, Amps, and Effects for All Styles

by Stephen Davis

PLAYBACK+
Speed • Pitch • Balance • Loop

To access audio visit:
www.halleonard.com/mylibrary

Enter Code
8268-4532-8522-7976

ISBN 978-1-70515-649-0

Visit Hal Leonard Online at
www.halleonard.com

World headquarters, contact:
Hal Leonard
7777 West Bluemound Road
Milwaukee, WI 53213
Email: info@halleonard.com

In Europe, contact:
Hal Leonard Europe Limited
1 Red Place
London, W1K 6PL
Email: info@halleonardeurope.com

In Australia, contact:
Hal Leonard Australia Pty. Ltd.
4 Lentara Court
Cheltenham, Victoria, 3192 Australia
Email: info@halleonard.com.au

CONTENTS

INTRODUCTION

Guitar players love gear! We love to play it, look at it, research it, buy, sell, and trade it, listen to it, and discuss it. The number of guitars, effects, and amps available today is just staggering. On top of that, new products based on old tones and new ideas are constantly being released. But how do you find what you want inside the ever-expanding options out there?

I have spent over 30 years chasing the tones I want and helping others do the same. My background as a guitar player, guitar tech, live sound engineer, studio engineer, and educator has given me a unique perspective on guitar tone and gear. While doing this I have developed common ideas that exist throughout much of the gear world. This has helped me to create a language that allows us to speak about gear with some common terms.

Tone is extremely subjective. What I love, the next player might hate, and vice versa. My goal with this book is to help players find the tone they are searching for and be able to communicate with others about tone with some common language. If you can find at least one thing that helps make your tone a little better, find the right new piece, or tweak what you already have in your collection, then I deem this book a success. I hope you find all of the tips and information helpful.

YOUR HANDS

The most important thing in any guitar rig is **you**, the player. Nothing can make you sound better than practicing and becoming a better musician.

People always say that "tone is in the hands." Well, that is correct—to some degree. We look up to great players because they sound great, and they usually have great gear. Most pros have spent their lifetime practicing their instrument and searching for the right gear to help them create their art. Their playing is the reason they sound unique, no matter what gear they are using.

Years ago, I was a partner in a small guitar shop in Nashville, Tennessee. One day, Billy Gibbons came in and hung out for about an hour. While he was there, another customer was playing a Les Paul-style guitar into a Marshall amp. When I walked into the amp room with Billy, the customer stopped playing. He then looked at Mr. Gibbons, handed him the guitar, and said "Here, I am just playing your licks anyway." Billy started to play the rig without turning a single knob, and it immediately sounded like him. The low end of the amp even changed drastically due to his playing. He was his sound; the gear was just his way of letting it be heard.

Gear is one of the major parts of the equation for achieving great tone. The guitars, effects, accessories, and amplifiers we use help us find our own sound. The search for tone is much like the quest to become a better musician; it is never-ending. Always remember to enjoy the journey.

ABOUT THE AUDIO

All recordings are done using a Universal Apollo interface and recorded into Logic Pro X. There is no processing done with any of the tracks after they are recorded. When recordings are used to help compare gear, the tracks are recorded direct and then re-amped with an active Radial re-amp box into the featured gear, if possible. This helps take out all as many variables as possible, therefore making the comparisons focused on the featured gear. The rest of the gear is listed by chapter.

The parts that I play are simple and meant to showcase the gear, not my playing. I hope you find this approach helpful. To access these recordings, go to **www.halleonard.com/mylibrary** and input the code found on page 1 of this book.

CHAPTER 1
SUMMARY OF A GUITAR RIG

The term *guitar rig* describes everything that is used to create your sound. This includes your guitars, effects, amps, cabinets, speakers, and the accessories needed to make them work together. It can be broken down into individual parts, like an amp rig or a pedalboard rig. But a guitar rig refers to the sum of the parts, collected together.

Throughout this book, we will analyze the individual parts of a guitar rig to help you better understand them. This should not only help you make better choices with your gear purchases, but it should also help you get more out of what you already own and make better choices when building your rig.

One of the best pieces of advice I can give to all players, no matter their skill level, is **know your rig**. You should know what your gear is, the signal flow of your rig, how to program it if applicable, and how to trouble shoot it when it goes down. This will help you get the most out of every component of your rig.

"A chain is no stronger than its weakest link"; this is a perfect proverb to apply to a guitar rig. You can have an amazing rig built to achieve every tone you could ever think of. But if one 3" patch cable goes bad in the wrong spot, your entire rig can die. You should always use quality gear and keep it clean and maintained as much as possible. Remember, quality does not always mean expensive. There is some great gear out there for every budget.

For the purposes of this book, most of the gear used is actual hardware, not modeling. (Hardware refers to actual guitars, effects, multi-effects, amps, cabinets, etc.) This is not because one is better than the other. Both are very useful when used in the correct setting. It is because most of what is modeled is based on hardware, hence the term "modeling." If you understand how a real vintage Marshall amp works, it will be much easier to understand the modeling option. But with all the options in the modeling world, you could use a model of the same amp and change the sound so drastically that it no longer resembles the amp you are modeling. This way of achieving your desired tone is fine, but it is better to understand that your end result is nothing like a vintage Marshall tone. Knowing these things makes communication to others and finding your desired tone much easier.

CHAPTER 2
GUITARS

Guitars are the first thing in the tone equation most players think about. For many of us, the look and sound of guitars is what made us want to play. Whether it's Jimi Hendrix's Stratocasters, Zakk Wylde's Les Pauls, Jimmy Page's Telecasters, Tosin Abasi's 8-strings, or Pat Metheny's ES-175, they call out to us and make us want to play. It would take an entire book to list all the options for guitars. But we can look at some of the most popular options to help you understand why guitars sound the way they do. Understanding these basic ideas will help you pick the guitar that is best for your needs. Let's look at some of the major aspects that create an instrument.

GUITAR CONSTRUCTION OPTIONS

Body Wood

The type of wood that is used to make the body of an instrument is a major contributor to the tone. Here is a list of a few of the most common body woods and what they add to the tone of the guitar.

- Alder: lighter weight, balanced tone, commonly used in Fender-style guitars.

- Ash: lighter weight, balanced tone with increased highs, commonly used in Fender-style guitars.

- Basswood: lighter weight, warm tone with increased midrange, commonly used in shredder-style guitars.

- Mahogany: medium to heavy weight, full sound with increased sustain, commonly used in Gibson-style guitars.

- Koa: medium to heavy weight, similar tone to mahogany with increased highs.

- Maple: primarily used for the top or cap of a body, comes in multiple styles such as flame, quilt, and burl. Gibson Les Pauls are well known for their maple tops.

Neck Wood

The type of wood used to construct the neck of a guitar also influences the tone. Here are a few of the most common options.

- Maple: the most common wood used for necks, bright in tone. It comes in different grades of plain, flame, and birdseye. Maple is used for most guitars outside of Gibson-style guitars.

- Mahogany: warm and fat tone, most common in Gibson-style guitars.

- Rosewood: warm and fat tone, increase in lows and midrange, increase in sustain.

Fretboard Wood

The type of wood used for the fretboard influences the tone as well. While there are some guitars that use one piece of wood for the neck and fretboard, it is more common for them to be made from separate pieces of wood. The tonal characteristics of the wood are the same for either option.

- Maple: common in all style of guitars except Gibson-style, bright in tone. (Gibson has made some guitars with maple fretboards, but they are rare in comparison to rosewood and ebony builds.)

- Rosewood: common in all styles of guitars, warmer in tone.

- Ebony: common in all styles, tonally sits between the warmth of rosewood and the bright sound of maple.

Neck-to-Body Connection

The most common ways the neck and the body are connected are *bolt-on*, *set-neck*, or *neck-through*.

- Bolt-on neck guitars make the neck-to-body connection by simply bolting the pieces of wood together. This makes it possible to easily change necks if damage occurs or if you want a change in tone or size. The tonal aspect of a bolt-on neck is a brighter, snappier tone with less sustain that its counterparts. Fender Stratocasters and Telecasters are almost always bolt-on. (There are a few custom models that are not, but they are rare.)

Example of a bolt-on neck joint.

- Set-neck guitars make the connection by gluing the neck and body together. This makes it extremely difficult to change the neck. (While a set neck can be removed, it can result in serious damage to the rest of the instrument.) The tonal results are a warmer tone and more sustain than a bolt-on. The Gibson Les Paul is probably the most common set-neck guitar.

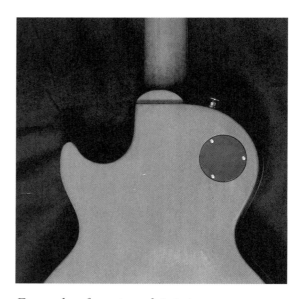

Example of a set-neck joint.

- Neck-through guitars use a piece of wood for the neck that extends all the way to the end of the body. The sides of the guitar are then glued onto the body part of the neck like a pair of wings. The tonal result is the most sustain and resonance out of the three designs. This design also gives the player easier access to the upper frets. These characteristics make it extremely popular with shredder-style guitars.

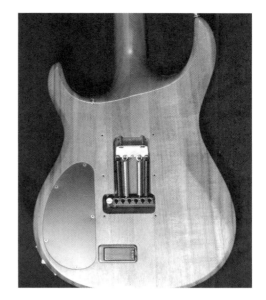

Example of a neck-through joint.

Scale Length

The *scale length* of a guitar is determined by measuring the distance from the edge of the nut, where it connects to the fretboard, to the center of the 12th fret, then doubling that number. For example, that measurement on a stock Fender Telecaster will be 12.75". If you double that number, you get 25.5", which is the standard scale length for most Fender guitars.

The most common scale lengths are 24.75", 25", and 25.5". While these are not all the available lengths by any means, they are the most common. As listed below, the change in scale length does change the playability of the instrument. While subtle, it is still worth mentioning.

Measuring the scale length.

- Gibson guitars primarily use a 24.75" scale length. This shorter scale length makes the guitar easier to play than the longer options and has a lower string tension. The tonal result is a stronger midrange but can create some muddiness in the low end.

- Paul Reed Smith guitars primarily use a 25" scale length. This in-between scale length results in a tone that is between a Fender- and Gibson-style guitar. The result is a more defined bottom end than the 24.75" scale and less top end than the 25.5".

- Fender guitars primarily use a 25.5" scale length. The longest of the three most popular scale is the most difficult to play and has a higher string tension than its shorter counterparts. This results in a more bell-like tone, more top end, and a more well-defined low end. 25.5" is the most common scale length used in most Strat-inspired guitars from builders like Ibanez, Jackson, Charvel, James Tyler, and Suhr.

Pickups

Pickups are magnets wound with copper wire. The magnet senses the vibration of the string and transmits that sound from the guitar to the amplifier. The type of magnet and the number of winds determine the tone and output of the pickup. The general rule is that more winds equal more output. Keep in mind that it is easier to get a better clean tone with lower output pickups and a better distorted tone with higher output pickups.

Pickups fall in two basic categories, *passive* and *active*. Most pickups are passive and do not require any type of power. Their tone is normally considered to be more vintage sounding and responsive to the player. But they do create more noise than their active counterparts. Passive pickups are responsible for all guitar sounds until the introduction of active pickups in the mid-1970s. All the audio recording clips are of passive pickups unless otherwise noted.

Example of single-coil pickups.

There are a handful of common designs when it comes to pickups. Each one has its own tone and place in the tonal spectrum.

Single-coil pickups tend to have a lower output and a cleaner tone. They do produce *60-cycle hum* due to interference with the surrounding electronic equipment. The recordings of the Stratocaster-style, Telecaster-style, chambered, baritone, and 12-string guitars all feature single-coil pickups.

Example of P-90 pickups.

P-90 pickups are single-coil pickups that are larger than a standard single-coil, yet smaller than a standard humbucker (see next page). Tonally, they tend to sound like a single-coil pickup on steroids. They do have the same issues with 60-cycle hum since they only have one coil.

 Track 1

Listen to Track 1 of a Gibson Les Paul Special with P90s. (To access this track and others, go to **www.halleonard.com/mylibrary** *and input the code found on pg. 1.)*

Example of humbucking pickups.

Humbuckers are pickups that combine two single-coils to make one pickup. The tonal result is normally a higher output and a more balanced EQ curve than single-coils. The combination of the two coils eliminates 60-cycle hum. The recordings of the Les Paul-style, the semi-hollow body, and the hollow body all feature humbuckers.

Example of mini-humbuckers.

Mini-humbuckers look like the baby brother of humbuckers. The design is very similar, except they are smaller. The tonal result is a loss of bottom end with an increase in midrange and highs. They can almost sound like a single-coil but are still somewhat aggressive. Since they are humbuckers, they do not have issues with 60-cycle hum.

 Track 2

Listen to Track 2 of a Gibson Les Paul Deluxe with mini-humbuckers.

Example of Filter'Tron pickups.

Filter'Tron pickups are most associated with Gretsch guitars. They are physically humbuckers, so they do not have the 60-cycle hum issue. But their tone is closer to the clarity of single-coils.

 Track 3

Listen to Track 3 of a Gretsch with Filter'Tron pickups.

Active pickups get their name from needing an active power supply for them to work. They are normally run on a single 9-volt battery that is mounted inside the body of the guitar. Active pickups have a distinct tone that often creates a brighter top end. The output is often higher, making them more aggressive than passive pickups. They are most often used by metal players, but you can find them in all kinds of music. EMGs are some of the most widely used active pickups out there.

 Track 4

Listen to Track 4 of an Ernie Ball Music Man Luke 1 with active EMG pickups.

Example of active pickups.

While these descriptions are of the most common choices of pickups, there are other aspects to think about. Humbuckers can be made into single-coil and P90-size pickups, called *stacks*. Also, single-coil and P90-style pickups can be made into humbucker-size pickups. You can also *coil-tap* some humbuckers, allowing only one side of the humbucker to be heard. This gives them the sound of a single-coil. While these are just a few options available, the basic concepts listed above apply to however you use the pickups.

Electronics

Electronics, like pickups, can be either passive or active. Most guitars are passive, using only volume and tone controls to shape the sound of the guitar.

Some, however, do use active circuits. This can be a circuit that is added to the passive volume and tone, like an *active mid-boost*. Or, it can be a fully active circuit that includes the volume and tone controls. As with active pickups, active electronics do require battery power.

Active electronics normally have more output than passive circuits, just like active pickups. While they do have some of the characteristics of active pickups, active electronics tend to not be sound as aggressive as active pickups. Some active preamp circuits can be bypassed with a switch, allowing you the best of both worlds. Although this is more common in bass guitars, it is seen in some electric guitars as well.

 Track 5

Listen to Track 5 for a clip of a bridge humbucker with an active mid-boost circuit. The first pass is with the control on 1; the second pass is on 10.

Bridge

Guitar *bridges* come in all styles. The two primary categories are those that have a *tremolo (whammy) bar* and those that do not.

Guitars that do not have a whammy bar tend to stay in tune better and usually have more sustain. They come in a few different styles that are normally associated with a particular style of guitar. The description of some of the most popular *fixed bridges* are listed with the guitar descriptions.

Guitars that have a whammy bar give the player the ability to adjust the pitch of what is being played. Whether it is the Eddie Van Halen dive bombs or the vocal-like manipulation of notes done by Jeff Beck, these techniques require a bridge with a whammy bar.

Keep in mind that if you bend a note on a guitar with a moving bridge, the guitar can potentially go out of tune. This means that if you bend a note and then play another note(s) while keeping the bend, the other note(s) will probably be out of tune. Also, *floating tremolos* tend to have less sustain than fixed bridges.

The most common tremolo system is the one used on a standard-style Stratocaster. These bridges can be set up to "float" above the body or be set up to rest on the body. While the floating option allows you to adjust the pitch being played up or down, the resting option tends to give the guitar more sustain.

Floyd Rose tremolos have been a standard for shredder-style guitars since the '80s. They are *double-locking tremolos* that replace a standard nut with a locking system and lock at the bridge as well. When set up correctly, Floyd Rose-equipped guitars are known for having extremely stable tuning. They are the most popular tremolo for shredders, allowing drastic use of the bar while remaining in tune.

Floyd Rose tremolo bridge.

Locking nut to be used with a Floyd Rose bridge.

Bigsby vibratos allow the manipulation of pitch up and down, but they use a *tune-o-matic bridge* as well. They are in a class all their own and are not considered floating bridges. They are often seen on Gretsch guitars but are also common on Les Pauls and Telecasters.

Bigsby vibrato bridge.

TYPES OF GUITARS

The following audio clips are done with each guitar starting on the bridge pickup and moving through each pickup selection in order, ending at the neck. The amp, cabinet, and microphones are not changed throughout the clips. While this might not deliver the best sound for the particular guitar recorded, it is the best way to hear the differences in the instruments.

Stratocaster Style

The standard Stratocaster is a double-cutaway guitar with three single-coil pickups, a five-way switch, bolt-on neck, 25.5" scale, and a tremolo. Stratocasters come with fixed bridges as well, but they are not as common. They are normally referred to as *hard tails*.

The standard electronics layout is one volume control, two tone controls, and a five-way pickup selector. The volume is global, the first tone knob controls the neck pickup, and the second tone knob controls the bridge and middle pickups. The five-way pickup selector gives these tonal options, starting from the option closest to the bridge: 1) bridge; 2) bridge and middle out of phase to reduce noise; 3) middle; 4) middle and neck out of phase to reduce noise; 5) neck.

 Track 6

Listen to Track 6 for a Stratocaster with five pickup options.

Fender Stratocaster.

Fender Telecaster.

Telecaster Style

The standard Telecaster is a single cutaway guitar with two single-coil pickups, a three-way switch, bolt-on neck, 25.5" scale, and a fixed bridge that surrounds the bridge pickup. Tremolo options are also available, but they are not as prominent.

The standard electronics layout is one volume control, one tone control, and a three-way pickup selector. The volume and tone knobs control both pickups. The three-way pickup selector gives these tonal options, starting from the option closest to the bridge: 1) bridge; 2) bridge and neck out of phase to reduce noise; 3) neck.

The guitar used for this recording has been modified with a four-position pickup selector, adding a setting with the bridge and neck pickup in phase. It does not cut out the 60-cycle hum, but it is a simple mod that adds one more tone to the instrument.

 Track 7

Listen to Track 7 for a Telecaster with four pickup options.

Gibson Les Paul.

Les Paul Style

The standard Les Paul is a single cutaway guitar with two humbucker pickups, a three-way switch, set neck, 24.75" scale, and a stop-bar tailpiece with a tune-o-matic bridge. Tremolo options are also available, but they are not as prominent.

The standard electronics layout is one volume and one tone control per pickup with a three-way pickup selector. The three-way pickup selector gives these tonal options, starting from the switch set to down: 1) bridge; 2) bridge and neck; 3) neck.

Track 8

Listen to Track 8 for a Les Paul with three pickup options.

Paul Reed Smith Style

Paul Reed Smith guitars come in all kinds of styles. They offer multiple bridges, pickup configurations, solid, semi-hollow, and chambered bodies, bolt-on and set necks, and different scale lengths. PRS guitars are well known for their 25" scale length, giving them a balance between the standards used by Fender and Gibson. (PRS does offer other scale lengths.)

The Paul Reed Smith used in this recording has two humbuckers, a five-way switch, set neck, and a PRS stop-tail bridge. This guitar does have a *piezo pickup* as well, but it is not used in the recording.

The electronics layout is one volume control, one tone control, and a five-way pickup selector. The volume and tone knobs control both pickups. The five-way pickup selector gives these tonal options, starting from the option closest to the bridge: 1) bridge humbucker; 2) bridge and neck (outer single-coils); 3) bridge and neck humbuckers; 4) bridge and neck (inner single-coils); 5) neck humbucker. Although there isn't a setting for one single-coil, this guitar is a great example of a coil-tapped sound.

 Track 9

Listen to Track 9 for a Paul Reed Smith with five pickup options.

Paul Reed Smith Custom 22.

Semi-Hollow Body

Semi-hollow body guitars are normally hollow on the sides with a block in the middle. (Some are only hollow in one area instead of two.) The block helps reduce feedback and increases sustain. The one in this recording is a Gibson ES-335. It has two humbucker pickups, a three-way switch, set neck, 24.75" scale, and a stop-bar tail piece with a tune-o-matic bridge.

The standard electronics layout is one volume and one tone control per pickup with a three-way pickup selector. The three-way pickup selector gives these tonal options, starting from the switch set to down: 1) bridge; 2) bridge and neck; 3) neck.

 Track 10

Listen to Track 10 for a Gibson ES-335 semi-hollow body with three pickup options.

Gibson ES-335.

Chambered

Chambered guitars have some of the body wood removed without being able to see this externally. This allows the guitar to sound more like a semi-hollow body and reduces the weight of the instrument. The one in this recording is a Telecaster-style guitar built from a Warmoth body and neck. It has three single-coil pickups wired like a Stratocaster, a five-way switch, bolt-on neck, 25.5" scale, and a standard Telecaster-style bridge.

The electronics layout is one volume control, one tone control, and a five-way pickup selector. The volume and tone knobs control both pickups. The five-way pickup selector gives these tonal options, starting from the option closest to the bridge: 1) bridge; 2) bridge and middle out of phase to reduce noise; 3) middle; 4) middle and neck out of phase to reduce noise; 5) neck.

While this is by no means what would be considered a standard guitar, it is a great example of a chambered body. The layout of this instrument is a cross between a Stratocaster and Telecaster style. This allows you to get some tonal variations of both instruments, making it extremely versatile.

 Track 11

Chambered Tele-style guitar.

Listen to Track 11 for a chambered Tele-style guitar with five pickup options.

Hollow Body

Hollow body guitars are very similar to acoustic guitars in that they are completely hollow inside. This results in a sound more like an acoustic guitar but causes the instrument to be more prone to feedback than the other designs. They are most often used for jazz but can be seen in all types of music. The electronics layout is one volume control, one tone control, and one floating humbucker. The guitar used in this recording is a Redentore Santissimo archtop.

 Track 12

Listen to Track 12 for a hollow body guitar.

Archtop guitar made by Redentore.

Danelectro Baritone.

Baritone

Baritone guitars are tuned lower than standard-tuned guitars. Most players tune them B–E–A–D–F♯–B, which is a perfect 4th lower than standard tuning. Some players do prefer tuning down a perfect 5th to A–D–G–C–E–B. This does require baritone guitars to have a longer scale length. For example, the Vintage Baritone by Danelectro has a 29.75" scale length. This allows greater stability for the lower tuning.

The Danelectro Vintage Baritone, which is used for the recording example, is set up as follows. The electronics layout is one volume control, one tone control, and a three-way pickup selector. The volume and tone knobs control both pickups. The pickups are two *lipstick-style* single-coils. The three-way pickup selector gives these tonal options, starting from the option closest to the bridge: 1) bridge; 2) bridge and neck out of phase to reduce noise; 3) neck.

 Track 13

Listen to Track 13 for a Danelectro Baritone with three pickup options.

Danelectro 12-String.

 Track 14

Listen to Track 14 for a Danelectro 12-String with three pickup options.

12-String Guitars

Twelve-string guitars are most often set to standard tuning. Each one of the six strings is then doubled for a total of 12. The bottom E, A, D, and G strings are doubled with a string one octave higher, while the top B and E strings are doubled with strings of the same pitch. This results in a very full sound with a natural chorusing effect.

For our purposes, we'll look at a Danelectro 12-string, which is used in the recording. The electronics layout is one volume control, one tone control, and a three-way pickup selector. The volume and tone knobs control both pickups. The pickups are two lipstick-style single-coils. The three-way pickup selector gives these tonal options, starting from the option closest to the bridge: 1) bridge; 2) bridge and neck out of phase to reduce noise; 3) neck.

Gear used for recording:

Amp: 1964 Fender Vibrolux Reverb

Cabinet: Petersen 1x12, open-back

Speaker: Celestion Alnico Cream, 90-watt

Microphones: Shure SM57, Royer 121

CHAPTER 3
AMPLIFIERS

Guitar amplifiers normally fall into four major categories: *tube*, *solid-state*, *hybrid*, and *modeling*.

TUBE AMPS

Tube amps are used by most players. They use vacuum tubes in the *preamp* and *power amp* sections to create their tone. Although there are a multitude of options available, we can break them down into three basic tonal characteristics of popular amps. These are *Fender-style* amps, *Vox-style* amps, and *Marshall-style* amps. You can see a great example of this concept in the Strymon Iridium pedal. It offers three different amp models designed after a Fender Deluxe Reverb, a Vox AC30, and a Marshall Plexi. (More on modelers later.)

While this seems limited to some players, think of amps as colors in a painting. There are three primary colors in our spectrum of sight. These colors are red, yellow, and blue. All the other colors we see are brought about by the combining of these three primary colors. If we approach tube amps the same way, we can compare the large selection of amps available.

Let's look at the three primary types of tube amps. (Each amp is recorded with three passes. The volume is turned from approximately 3 to 5 and then to 8 to show the differences in *break-up*. The rest of the controls on the amp are not changed.)

Fender

Fender amps are primarily known for their clean tone, but also have a beautiful *gain* when turned up. They primarily use 6L6 tubes in their power amp sections. The Fender Deluxe and Deluxe Reverb amps are considered the most recorded guitar amps in history. These models use the smaller 6V6 power amp tubes. While Fender does use EL84 tubes in some of their smaller amps, like the Blues Junior series, their sound is primarily associated with the 6L6 and 6V6 power amp tubes.

Fender amps are known for having a lot of headroom, big low end, and a clear top end to their tone. This makes them extremely popular for clean tones. Due to this, many players use Fender amps as pedal platforms. This means that they dial in a great sounding clean tone from the amp and use pedals to add overdrive and other effects. This is very useful when you must cover a wide variety of sounds in a setting such as a cover band.

Randall Smith of Mesa Boogie started his company by modifying Fender amps. This is part of the reason that Boogie amps are well known for having a lot of bottom end in their tone.

 Track 15

Listen to Track 15 of a 1964 Fender Vibrolux Reverb with a Tone Tubby Alnico Red 10" speaker.

Fender Vibrolux Reverb amplifier.

Vox AC30 amplifier, top view and then front.

Vox

Vox amps are well known for their clean tones and edge of break-up tones. Their most popular amp, the AC30 has four EL84 tubes in the power amp section. The smaller version, the AC15, only uses two EL84 tubes. Due to vintage Vox amps being considered unstable by most players and technicians, many boutique companies have done their own versions of the famous amplifiers. The Matchless C30 series is one of the most popular boutique versions of the AC30.

Vox amps have a unique top end that breaks up different than other tube amps. They are also known for not having as much bottom end as a Fender or midrange as a Marshall. The unique top end of a Vox style amp can easily be heard in many of Brad Paisley's recordings. His love of Teles and Vox amps help to contribute to his bright guitar tone.

 Track 16

Listen to Track 16 of a 1965 Vox AC30 with a vintage Celestion Alnico Silver speaker.

Marshall

Marshall amps are well known for their natural overdrive but can also be dialed in for a wonderful clean tone. Their tonal center is more pronounced in the midrange than Fender and Vox amps. They primarily use EL34 tubes in the power amp section, although some amps do use EL84s or 5881s. The 100-watt Super Lead, nicknamed the "Plexi," due to its plexiglass front panel, is considered one of the holy grails of guitar tone. One of the most popular recordings of the Plexi is Jimi Hendrix's *Live at Woodstock*.

Its predecessor, the JTM45, is often considered as influential as the Plexi. The JTM45 was originally released in 1962, three years prior to the first Plexi. These amps use two 5881s in the power amp section and are rated at 45 watts. They are known for not having as much gain as the Super Lead. The 2x12 combo version included tremolo in the circuit, making it sound slightly different. The combo is nicknamed the "Bluesbreaker," due to Eric Clapton using it with John Mayall and the Bluesbreakers.

Marshall is also known for 18- and 20-watt amps that use EL84s in the power amp section. These smaller amps sound great and overdrive quickly, but they do not have the headroom that the larger amps do. Many of today's amp companies got their start by modifying Marshall amps to have more gain. Mike Soldano, Paul Rivera, and Reinhold Bogner are just three great examples of today's amp designers who are well known for modifying amps for rock stars before releasing their own designs.

Marshall Super Lead amplifier.

 Track 17

Listen to Track 17 of a 1972 Marshall Super Lead into a Petersen open-back, 1x12 cabinet with a 90-watt Celestion Alnico Cream speaker.

SOLID-STATE AMPS

Solid-state amps use transistors instead of tubes to create their sound. While they are not as popular among players as tube amps, they do have their place. Solid-state amps are normally cheaper, lighter, and more reliable than tube amps. They also tend to have more headroom and are easier to work on.

Solid-state amps do not have the same natural overdrive and compression that tube amps do when turned up. Many players who use solid-state amps recreate these missing elements with pedals. Some players, especially those playing traditional jazz, often do not want the natural overdrive and compression created by tube amps. They tend to rely on the pure clean tone created by solid-state amps.

Solid-state amps are common in all types of music. Wes Borland of Limp Bizkit used a Roland JC120 for his live clean tone. The Gibson L5 Lab Series amp was often used by B.B. King, as well as by Ty Tabor for the first three King's X albums. Jazz players are well known for using Polytone amps for their big clean tone. Also, many players on the Nashville, Tennessee "Lower Broad" circuit use the Boss Katana series amps for their reliability, light weight, and consistent tone.

Notice that while the tube amps break up more when they are turned up, the solid-state amp stays cleaner longer. This is very useful when you need a loud, clean tone.

Boss Katana amplifier, top view and then front.

 **Track 18**

Listen to Track 18 of a Boss Katana with its stock speaker for a solid-state clean tone.

HYBRID AMPS

Hybrid amps use a combination of tube and solid-state design. Some of the most popular hybrid amps were built by Music Man. They use EL34 or 6L6 tubes for the power amp section, and either a single 12AX7 or all solid state components in the preamp section. The layout depends on the year the amp was made. Leo Fender, of Fender Musical Instruments fame, was one of the designers in these amps. They were primarily designed to be loud, clean amps, while adding some warmth from the power amp tubes not found in solid state amps. There are other hybrid amps, but Music Man made some of the most popular ones.

Due to the scarcity of hybrid amps when compared to their tube, solid state, and modeling counterparts, they are not used as often by guitarists. They are very popular with traditional country players and steel players for their bright clean tone.

MODELING AMPS

Modeling amps use software programs to produce the sounds of real amplifiers. These are either strictly software-based and require a computer or have their own hardware for processing. Many of today's players use modeling amps due to cost, consistent tone, lack of need for dedicated guitar cabinets, and the ability to have a multitude of tonal options in one place.

Many of today's touring musicians use modeling amps. The most popular are from Line 6, Kemper, and Fractal Audio. They normally send a signal directly to the engineers instead of having to place a microphone on a speaker cabinet. This helps keep the stage volume down and their tone consistent from night to night, due to the room not playing a factor in the sound.

Studio players, especially those in smaller project studios, use modelers for endless options, the ability to record without the volume of the amp, and the lack of needing to carry a stack of amps to a session. (We will address the tone of modelers in Chapter 5.)

ATTENUATORS

Although *attenuators* are not amplifiers, they are often used in conjunction with tube amps. Attenuators are pieces of gear that are placed between an amp and speaker. These connections must be done with speaker cables, not instrument cables. They act like a master volume for your amp. This allows you to turn up the overall volume of your amp, therefore saturating the power amp tubes to create natural overdrive and compression and turn the volume down with the attenuator.

Attenuators can be a life saver when used correctly. The biggest mistake most players make when using one is thinking they will get the exact same tone from their amp when they lower the volume on the attenuator.

First, your speakers will respond differently because they are not being pushed as hard due to the decrease in volume. When an amp is turned up, the speakers must physically move more. This changes the overall tone of the speakers, causes them to compress, and allows them to break up and create natural distortion. When an attenuator is used to turn down the volume, these characteristics of the speakers change. They have to move less, allowing them to break up and compress less, resulting in a cleaner overall sound.

Second, the EQ of what we hear changes in relation to the volume we hear it. This is described by the *Fletcher Munson curve*. The basic idea on the Fletcher Munson curve is that we hear more midrange at lower volumes and less midrange at higher volumes. While this is very far from the correct scientific definition, it will help with our explanation here. If we turn a 100-watt amplifier up to 10 without using an attenuator, what we hear will have fewer mids and more lows and highs than if the volume was on 2. Now, if we add the attenuator and bring the overall volume down to sound like the amp is on 2, we will hear an increase in the mids and a decrease in the lows and highs. This is all due to the Fletcher Munson Curve.

So, how do you fix this? First, if possible, dial in your rig exactly the way you plan on using it. Try not to add an attenuator to your rig after you have rehearsed without one for your gig. Second, you should always be willing to change your settings. If you attenuate your sound and lose the big bottom end you love, try to dial it back in with the EQ on your amp or with an EQ pedal. This might not fix the issue entirely, but it can help.

 Track 19

Listen to Track 19 of a Marshall Super Lead using a Weber Mass, first bypassed, then turned on. The settings on the amp are not changed between the two recordings.

Weber Mass attenuator.

EFFECTS LOOPS

Effects loops are found in all kinds of amps. They are most often seen in amps producing a lot of gain or with more than one channel available. But they are also seen in cleaner, single-channel amps.

An effects loop is an insert point between the preamp and power amp section of an amp. This is most often used to insert effects at this point. Most players place modulation, delay, and reverb in the effects loop and run the other pedals into the front of the amp. This allows for the effects in the loop to sound cleaner than if they were placed in the front.

Effects loops normally have a send and a return jack that are normally located on the back of the amp. The cable connected to the send goes to the input of the first pedal you want in your loop, and the return is connected to the output of the last pedal in the loop. While most loops are set to instrument level, some are set to line level and can only be used with pedals that offer line level. This is thoroughly discussed in Chapter 13 on delays.

Example of an effects loop.

Effects loops can work in *series* or *parallel*. A series effects loop breaks the signal at the send and return and runs 100% of the dry signal into the effects in the loop. This is the most basic version of the two designs and the most common. A parallel effects loop splits the path between the preamp and power amp sections of an amplifier and usually has a mix knob. The dry signal stays dry, and the effects are then mixed in with the mix knob. This obviously offers more versatility than the series option. If the effects in the loop offer a mix option on them, you can get a similar effect in a series by adjusting the mix of the effects. Both options are great, it just depends on your personal preference.

NOTES ON AMPLIFIERS

There are a few things to keep in mind when using real amps:

1. Always use a speaker cable when connecting an amp to an internal speaker within a combo or connecting a head to a cabinet. If you use an instrument cable to make this connection, you can damage your amp.

2. When using a tube amp, make sure your amp is connected to a speaker or some type of load box. Playing into a tube amp that is not connected to a load (a speaker or load box are both considered *loads*) can damage your amp.

3. Make sure you have the proper voltage when turning your amp on. Most modern amps run on 120 volts, so this is normally not an issue. But vintage amps can be a lot pickier. A voltage regulator like a Brown Box or a Variac can help you achieve the desired voltage. Running voltage too high or too low can damage your amp. Be sure to check what your amp runs on to optimize the tone and lifespan.

4. Unless you know what you are doing, do not work on your own amp. The voltage held inside of an amp can be very dangerous, even when they are unplugged. Take your amp to a reputable repair person when you need work done.

Gear used for recording:

Guitar: Strat-style, bridge single-coil pickup

Amp: Listed per clip

Cabinet: Listed per clip

Speaker: Listed per clip

Microphones: Shure SM57, Royer 121

CHAPTER 4

GUITAR CABINETS AND SPEAKERS

The speaker is usually the last thing in your guitar rig. The speaker and the cabinet that it is in make a large contribution to your tone. Let's look at some of the most popular styles.

CABINETS

Guitar cabinets come in all shapes and sizes. From the 1x8 (meaning one 8" unit) speaker cabinet in the Fender Champ combo, to the classic Marshall 4x12, there is something out there for everyone. Guitar cabinets are exactly that, cabinet style enclosures for your speakers. When dealing with combo amps, the cabinet includes the amp as well.

The size, material, and build style all make a difference in the sound of a cabinet. There are a multitude of options available of all different styles. Since there are too many for us to discuss here, let's break it down to the three most common styles of cabinet designs. These include *open-back*, *closed-back*, and *ported*. Let's look at all three.

Open-Back Cabinets

Open-back cabinets have an open or partially open-back panel. This design is almost always seen in combo amps to help keep the amp from getting too hot. (There are some combo amps with closed backs. They are more common in solid state amps than tube amps.)

This open-back design projects your sound out of the rear of the cabinet as well as the front. This allows the people behind your cabinet to hear you better than the closed or ported options. It also gives a less directional sound that can feel like it is surrounding you. The tonal result is an increase in midrange and highs with a decrease in bottom end.

An open-back cabinet also allows you to mic the front and back of the cabinet. This can be great for recording purposes since it gives you two different sounds from your speaker. Make sure that the mic you have on the back of the cabinet is out of phase with the one on the front, or you will have serious phasing issues.

 Track 20

Listen to Track 20 for a Petersen 1x12 cabinet with an open-back. This clip has one mic on the front.

 Track 21

Listen to Track 21 for a Petersen 1x12 cabinet with an open-back. This clip has one SM57 on the front and one on the back. This pass has the phase reversed on the rear mic. This is standard for recordings of this style.

 Track 22

*Listen to Track 22 for a Petersen 1x12 cabinet with an open-back. This clip has one SM57 on the front and another on the back. The phase has **not** been reversed on the rear mic. This is what you want to avoid.*

Petersen open-back cabinet with a single 12" speaker, front view.

Petersen open-back cabinet with a single 12" speaker, rear view.

Closed-Back Cabinets

Closed-back cabinets seal off the cabinet so that your sound is only coming out of the front. The result is a more directional sound. This can result in a smaller "sweet spot" on stage where you can best hear your sound. It also keeps your sound from being projected out of the back of the cabinet.

The tonal result is an increase in low end and a stronger midrange than its open-back counterpart. Therefore, you see most players who want a lot of low end in their sound end up normally using closed-back cabinets. Hard rock and metal players are well known for using closed-back cabinets for this reason.

 **Track 23**

Listen to Track 23 of the same Petersen 1x12 cabinet with a closed back.

Petersen closed-back cabinet with a single 12" speaker.

Ported Cabinets

Ported cabinets have a small opening in the front or back of the cabinet. While they are not as common in the guitar world as open- or closed-back designs, they are still readily available.

They tend to sound like the closed-back designs, but not exactly. The overall tone of the cabinet depends on how the designer tuned the port. Most are used to increase low end and tend to be in smaller cabinets.

Pacific ported cabinet with a single 12" speaker.

 **Track 24**

Listen to Track 24 of a ported Pacific 1x12 cabinet with the same speaker as the previous clips.

SPEAKERS

Since there are thousands of speakers to choose from, it would be impossible to address them all here. Let's look at some of the main properties of dealing with them.

Cabinets either contain a single speaker or multiple speakers. The most common single speaker designs are a 1x10 and a 1x12. The most common multi-speaker cabinets are 2x10, 4x10, 2x12, and 4x12. Multi-speaker cabinets contain either the same speaker throughout (*matched*), or different speakers (*mismatched*). Mismatched speaker cabinets allow you more tonal options by placing a mic on either one for the individual sound, or both to blend the sounds.

The use of matched or mismatched speakers is a preference of the builder or the player. Most amp and cabinet builders use matched speakers. Marshall is known for using matched speakers in the amps and cabinets, while Matchless is known for often placing a mismatched pair of speakers in their amps and cabinets.

IMPEDANCE

When you look on the output of your amp, or the input of your cabinet, you should see a label with a number and this symbol: Ω. This is the *impedance* of your amp's output or cabinet's input measured in ohms. If your amp has multiple speaker outs, they should all be labeled individually. Most guitar amps and cabinets use 4, 8, or 16 ohms. (The 4x10 Fender Bassman, which runs at 2 ohms, is probably the most popular exception.) For our reasons here, let's look at how to deal with this.

First and foremost, you want to match the impedance of your amp and cabinet if possible. This means you should plug a 4-ohm output from your amp into a 4-ohm cabinet, 8 into 8, 16 into 16, etc. This will allow the amp to run exactly how it is designed and is the safest way for it to be used.

If you can't match the impedance, it is best to run a lower impedance number into a higher impedance number. Running a 4-ohm head into an 8-ohm cabinet, or 8 into 16, is a prime example. This will normally lower the overall output of the amp and decrease the lows and highs produced. While this is considered safe, you should contact the manufacturer of your amp before connecting any cabinet that is not the same impedance. Connecting a tube amp with a higher impedance number to a cabinet with a lower impedance number, e.g., 8 into 4, 16 into 8, can cause damage to your amp. I highly recommend **not** doing this.

Weber Z-Matcher impedance box.

Weber Speakers makes a wonderful little box called a Z-Matcher that is designed to fix these issues. This piece of gear goes between your amp and cabinet and matches impedances to make sure your amp is running safe. This ensures you are getting the best tone possible.

There are four different ways to determine the impedance of a cabinet. Let's look at them.

1. The simplest setup has one only one speaker. The impedance should be labeled on the speaker.

2. The next design is running speakers in series. This is most often seen in a cabinet with two speakers. Wiring a two-speaker cabinet in series with 8-ohm speakers results in 2 x 8 = 16.

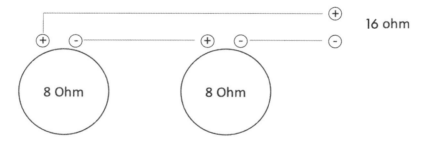

3. Our third design runs parallel. As with the series design, this is most often seen in a cabinet with two speakers. Wiring a two-speaker cabinet in parallel with 8-ohm speakers results in 2 x 8 = 4.

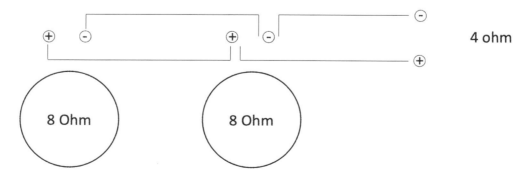

4. The final wiring option is series/parallel. This combines both series and parallel wiring. This is most often seen in cabinets with four speakers. Wiring a four-speaker cabinet in series/parallel with 8-ohm speakers results in 4 x 8 = 8.

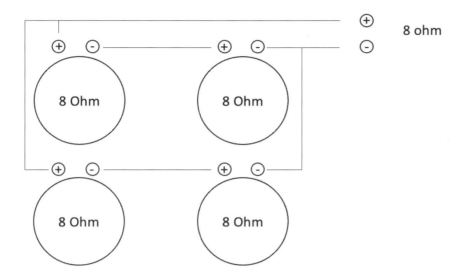

WATTAGE

The *wattage* rating of a speaker lets you know how much power the speaker can handle. The basic rule is that you don't want to plug an amp with a higher wattage rating than your speaker. So plugging a 30-watt amp into a 50-watt speaker is completely fine. But plugging a 50-watt amp into a 30-watt speaker can create problems. Running more power into a speaker than it is rated for can cause serious damage to the speaker.

If you are running more than one speaker with your amp, you should multiply the wattage of the lowest-rated speaker by the number of speakers in your cabinet to determine the wattage of the cabinet. This means that if you are running a 2x12 cabinet with two 30-watt speakers, the cabinet is rated at 60 watts (30 x 2 = 60). But if you are running a 25-watt speaker and a 30-watt speaker in a 2x12 cabinet, the cabinet is rated at 50 watts (25 x 2 = 50).

While it seems that it is completely safe to match the wattage output of your amp to the handling capabilities of your speaker(s), this isn't always the case. Running a 100-watt amp on 10 into a cabinet rated at 100 watts can blow your speakers. The safest way to match your amp and speakers is to have your cabinet rated higher than the output of the amp. As with everything involving tone, it is entirely up to your ears.

Gear used for recording:

Guitar: Strat-style, bridge single-coil pickup

Amp: 1972 Marshall Super Lead

Cabinet: Listed per clip

Speaker: Celestion Alncio Cream, 90-watt

Microphone: Shure SM57

CHAPTER 5
MODELING AND GOING DIRECT

Going direct with your guitar signal is as common in today's world as using real amps and effects. The use of stand-alone modelers, software modelers, and speaker modeling load boxes have changed the face of the guitar world. Units like the Line 6 Helix, Fractal Axe-FX, and Kemper Profiler, along with countless software options, allow players to have a multitude of amps, cabinets, speakers, effects, microphones, and room simulations that would not be available any other way.

One common thread among modelers of all kinds is that they almost always model gear that already exists. There are very few models that aren't based on gear that doesn't already exist in hardware. So if you understand the gear that models are based on, you can get more out of your modeler.

For example, let's say you want to dial up a classic rock guitar sound. A common signal path would be a Tube Screamer overdrive, a Memory Man delay, a Marshall Super Lead, and a 4x12 cabinet with Celestion Greenbacks. This can deliver a great classic rock guitar tone. But what if you want less midrange in your tone? Some people would place an EQ in line and cut the midrange back. While this can work, if you understand that a Tube Screamer has a large bump in the midrange, you will know that replacing the pedal with something like a Timmy might be a better idea than just cutting the midrange that is being produced by your choice of overdrive pedal.

Another example would be if you want to dial up a heavily distorted, modern metal tone. If we look at the three basic ideas of tube amps, we can almost guarantee that a Vox-style amp will not work. This gives us Marshall- and Fender-style amps to start with. Also, since we probably want a lot of bottom end, we should focus on closed-back or possibly ported cabinets instead of open-back. While this can be discovered by trial and error, using the concepts laid out in this book can help you dial in your tone quicker and more efficiently.

Modeling gear is not the same as the gear that it actually models. A model of something is never the exact same as the original. But modelers can be as good or better for the job than their hardware counterparts, depending on the application.

One important aspect of modeling is that you can create rigs that are not physically possible with hardware. Depending on the modeling unit or software that you use, you can do things such as run a Marshall Plexi with 6v6 tubes into a 1x8 cabinet. Running 6v6's is not possible with a real Plexi. Not to mention that you could blow up a 1x8 speaker if you turned the volume past 2. But this is completely possible in the modeling world.

Another important aspect of modeling is that it allows you to go direct in both live and studio settings. The result is being able to achieve tones without speaker cabinets that would normally require turning up loud amps. This is extremely beneficial if you want to record when other people are in your household or if your neighbors don't want to listen to what you are doing. There are also venues and tours that do not allow speakers on stage, so modeling is your only option.

Modeling rigs and hardware rigs do not respond the same. Each one responds to your hands differently, just like different guitars, amps, and effects respond differently. Again, there really is not a better option. Your best choice is to get to know both and use what you need in the proper setting. There are countless debates about which option is better: modeling or traditional hardware? The truth is that they both have their own pros and cons. If you look at everything as a tool to create music, then it is easier to realize that they are all equal.

To show that they all have their place and can sound great, let's listen to a few different designs using the same style of rig with four different styles. (The recordings in this chapter are done with the volume at approximately 3 and then 5. This is to show how the break-up changes with increases in volume. The controls are set to halfway on all the EQs to help show the differences.)

This audio clip is done with a Fender '59 Bassman Reissue loaded with a 10A125 speaker from Weber Speakers. The microphones are a Shure SM57 and a Royer 121.

 **Track 25**

Listen to Track 25 for a Fender '59 Bassman Reissue amplifier.

Fender '59 Bassman Reissue amplifier, front view and then top.

This audio clip is done with the same '59 Bassman RI into a Universal Audio OX speaker modeling load box. The head is a tube amp, but the cabinet and microphones are modeling. The cab model is the 410 Bman, which is based on a vintage 1959 Fender Bassman. The microphone models are based on a Shure SM57 and a Royer 121.

 Track 26

Listen to Track 26 for the Bassman Reissue using the OX for speaker and microphone modeling.

Universal Audio OX speaker modeling load box.

This audio clip is done with a Line 6 HX Stomp XL. This is a stand-alone modeling unit. The amp is set to a model of a vintage Fender Bassman combo and its 4x10 speakers. The microphone models are based on a Shure SM57 and a Royer 121.

 Track 27

Listen to Track 27 for a Line 6 HX Stomp XL.

Line 6 HX Stomp XL.

This audio clip is done with Amp Designer in Logic Pro X. This is a software-based modeling unit. The amp is set to a model of a vintage Fender Bassman combo and its 4x10 speakers. The microphone models are based on a Shure SM57 and a Royer 121.

 **Track 28**

Listen to Track 28 for Amp Designer in Logic Pro X.

As you can hear, all the tones are very similar. There isn't a better or worse, only different. The main difference is that the recording using modeling sounds more polished than the amp on its own. This is primarily due to way that the models were created. The influence of the room they were recorded in, the recording gear used, and the way they were modeled makes a big difference in the tone.

The *frequency response* allowed by modelers also makes a big difference in the tone when compared to an amp. Since modelers are not limited to 6-string guitars, they are normally designed to process the entire spectrum of what we can hear from 20hz to 20k. Standard guitar amps, however, are much more limited in their frequency response. You can alter this with the EQ in your modelers to make them sound more like a traditional amp. There is no added EQ in these recordings to help emphasize the differences in the gear.

Finally, you do not have to use only hardware or modeling in your rig. It is very common to use traditional amps, cabinets, and effects along with stand-alone modelers and software modelers. The two worlds work great together. The only limit is your willingness to learn what works for you.

CHAPTER 6

BUILDING A PEDALBOARD

Guitar players love pedals! These fun little boxes help guitarists create tones from the traditional to ones that morph the instrument into something that doesn't even resemble the sound of a guitar. Let's look at what is needed to build a pedalboard to meet your needs.

THE PEDALBOARD

Pedalboards are exactly that. They are platforms to mount you pedals, power supplies, and cables to help keep your rig organized, sounding great, and easy to use.

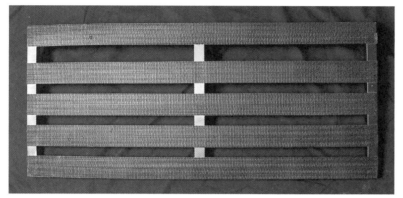

Pedaltrain board.

There are multiple companies out there that build pedalboards. One of the most popular companies out there is Pedaltrain. They build multiple boards ranging from the Nano (14" x 5.5" x 1.4") to the Terra 42 (42" x 14.5" x 3.5"). The size is only relative to how much space you need for the pedals that you would like to use.

The primary way players mount their pedals is with Velcro. While standard Velcro does work, most players prefer the stability of 3M Dual Lock. It helps keep your gear mounted to the pedalboard, which in turn helps prevent damage to your gear.

POWER SUPPLIES

Power supplies are an essential element as well. While some pedalboards have built-in power supplies, most are designed to be used with third-party supplies. These are often, but not always, mounted under the board. Most Pedaltrain boards have enough space underneath to mount the most common power supplies on the market. They also offer mounting brackets to help secure them. It is common to put power supplies on the top of smaller or flat-style boards.

Power supplies come in two primary designs: *isolated* and *non-isolated*. Some power supplies have an isolated and a non-isolated section.

Isolated power supplies allow a fixed voltage and current for each individual output. The result is like using a dedicated power supply for each individual pedal. Each output acts independently from the others. For this reason, most players prefer isolated power supplies. Isolated power supplies are also known for being quieter than non-isolated ones.

Non-isolated power supplies, while often cheaper, do not have dedicated power for each pedal connected. They use a *daisy chain* design to distribute power to the pedals. This can be done with an actual daisy chain cable used to connect all the power inputs on your pedals. Or, it can be done with individual cables that draw from one common power output.

While the voltage is fixed, the current is set at a higher amount and is distributed to the pedals in the order they are connected. This can cause the pedals at the end of the daisy chain to not receive the correct power. For example, let's say you connect five pedals in a power chain that each require 250 milliamps of power for a total of 1250 milliamps needed. If the power supply only delivers 1100 milliamps, the first four pedals in the power chain will receive the needed 250 milliamps. But the last pedal will only receive the remaining 150 milliamps. This is due to electricity always following the path of least resistance. The result is that the last pedal might not power up correctly, at all, or have an increased level of noise.

Picking out the correct power supply for your pedalboard is directly dependent on the pedals that you want to use. While most pedals require 9 volts and up to 200 milliamps of power, some require much more. For example, while the Ibanez Tube Screamer requires 9V and 7.5mA, the Strymon TimeLine requires 9V and a minimum of 300mA. Other pedals, such as the Electro-Harmonix Deluxe Memory Man, require 24V and 45mA. The key is to find out what your pedals need and use the power supply that best suits them. Always be sure and check the power requirements for your pedals. Connecting a pedal to the incorrect power can cause the pedal to not work or even damage the pedal if the voltage is too high.

Not having the correct power to a pedal, especially a digital one, can cause a pedal to not turn on at all, randomly switch on and off, have noise issues, and/or not function properly. If you are experiencing any of these issues, check the power you are using for that pedal.

Below is an audio clip of the noise created by digital pedals not receiving enough current. The pedals work properly, but the underlying digital noise is constant. The noise can easily be fixed by using the correct power supply.

 Track 29

Listen to Track 29 for digital noise.

MXR Iso-Brick power supply.

Some of the most popular isolated power supplies on today's market are the Truetone CS12, the Voodoo Labs Pedal Power 3, the MXR Iso-Brick, and the Strymon Zuma. While all of these are high-quality supplies, they each have slightly different specs. Make sure you have the right number of outputs, the correct voltage, the correct current (your current output can be higher than needed and be completely safe for most pedals, while the voltage must match exactly), and that it fits on or under your board of choice. If you have any questions about the current and voltage needed for a pedal, contact the builder before powering up your pedal.

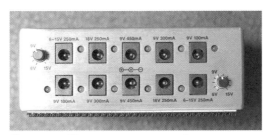

Strymon Zuma power supply.

CABLING

Almost all pedals are connected by standard 1/4" instrument cables. Some pedals can use stereo 1/4" cables, but they are not very common. Building cables to length is the optimum way to connect your pedals. However, not all guitarists are able to do that. So using premade cables is also a good option. Whatever you do, try to keep the slack to a minimum and use high-quality cables. Your rig is only as strong as its weakest link, so avoid using low-quality cables if possible.

Cables do break or become intermittent at times. Most issues are created by moving the cables and the plugging in and unplugging of pedals. The best way to avoid this is to keep your pedalboard clean, your pedals mounted, and leave the connections alone when you don't need to change them. Broken cables will not pass any signal at all, so they are obvious. Intermittent cables often cause a crackling noise that makes your pedalboard unusable.

Here is a clip of the noise created by an intermittent cable connecting two pedals.

 Track 30

Listen to Track 30 for an intermittent cable.

CASES

Most pedalboards, like the ones from Pedaltrain, come with cases. There are two primary types of cases. First is the soft case (figure 1). These cases allow for minimal protection but are lightweight and easy to carry. They are great for in-town gigs where you don't have to travel far with your gear. The second is a hard-shell case or road case (figure 2). These offer great protection but are much heavier. Hard-shell cases are the preference for touring musicians and most of those who gig regularly. While they are heavier, they offer a lot more protection for your gear.

Soft case for pedalboard.

Road case for pedalboard.

Most of today's guitarists shape their tone by using effects. You can make your guitar sound like almost anything imaginable with today's options of effects. For this book, we will focus on pedal effects. You can apply the same concepts to rack gear, plug-ins, and modelers. For example, if you understand what an actual Tube Screamer does, you can apply that to anything that models a Tube Screamer as well.

We will break down effects into a handful of categories in the following chapters. These include compression, drive, noise reduction, EQ, modulation, delay, reverb, filter, and other effects. While it is impossible to cover all the options available, this information should give you a good understanding of many of the effects being used today.

CHAPTER 7
OVERDRIVE, DISTORTION, FUZZ, AND BOOST

Primary Controls

- Volume or Level controls the overall output of the pedal.

- Gain, Drive, Distortion, or Fuzz controls the overall amount of these parameters. The more you turn this knob up, the more you will have to turn your volume control down to maintain the same volume when turning the pedal on or off.

- EQ, Tone, Filter, Bass, Mid, or Treble changes the overall tone of the pedal. These controls are often a simple tone knob but can have multiple options.

The main effect used by most guitar players is distorting their clean signal. Some players use their amps to get this desired sound while others use pedals. Most single-channel tube amps can be overdriven by turning up the volume. While this sounds amazing, it creates an issue with the volume often being too loud. Other players use multi-channel amps to create this sound. Most of today's players use pedals for these sounds.

Using pedals to get an overdriven tone is the most common, versatile, and cost-effective way of getting there. It is much cheaper to buy a new pedal than to buy another amp to get the new drive tone you want. This has helped lead to countless builders designing thousands of drive pedals. So how do you go about finding what is right for your needs? First, let's look at the four basic designs of drive pedals.

OVERDRIVE

Overdrive pedals are primarily used to create a unique overdriven tone. They can also be used to emulate the sound of an overdriven amp. These are often referred to as "amp in a box" pedals. Some classic examples are the Ibanez Tube Screamer, Klon Centaur, and Paul C. Audio or MXR Timmy pedals. (These overdrive pedals are not designed to emulate particular amps.)

 Track 31

Listen to Track 31 for an Ibanez Tube Screamer, first off and then on.

Ibanez Tube Screamer.

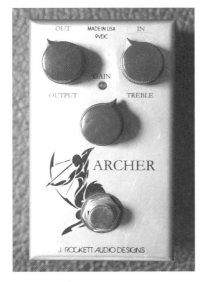

 Track 32

Listen to Track 32 for a Klon Centaur clone (Rockett Archer), first off and then on.

Rockett Archer.

 Track 33

Listen to Track 33 for a MXR Timmy, first off and then on.

MXR Timmy.

DISTORTION

Distortion is primarily used for more aggressive sounds. They tend to have more gain available than most overdrive pedals. They are also not designed to sound like amps, since the "amp in a box" style overdrive pedals are designed to emulate the natural overdrive of an amp. Some classic examples are the Rat, Boss DS-1, and Maxon SD-9.

Pro Co Rat.

 Track 34

Listen to Track 34 for a Pro Co Rat, first off and then on.

Boss DS-1.

 **Track 35**

Listen to Track 35 for a Boss DS-1, first off and then on.

Maxon SD-9.

 **Track 36**

Listen to Track 36 for a Maxon SD-9, first off and then on.

FUZZ

Fuzz pedal designs primarily use germanium or silicon transistors to create the sound and are often used for tones more aggressive than an overdrive or distortion. Fuzz pedals are common in all types of music from Jimi Hendrix to Jack White. Their aggressive and often powerful sound can help you achieve an overpowering tone. Some classic examples are a Germanium Fuzz Face, a Silicon Fuzz Face, and an Electro-Harmonix Big Muff.

*Dunlop Germanium
Fuzz Face Mini.*

 Track 37

Listen to Track 37 for a Dunlop Germanium Fuzz Face Mini, first off and then on.

*Dunlop Silicon
Fuzz Face Mini.*

 Track 38

Listen to Track 38 for a Dunlop Silicon Fuzz Face Mini, first off and then on.

Electro-Harmonix Big Muff.

 Track 39

Listen to Track 39 for an Electro-Harmonix Big Muff, first off and then on.

BOOST

Boost pedals are often designed to overdrive the front of a tube amp and/or increase volume for solos or important parts in a song. Boost pedals normally only have a light amount of gain available. Therefore, they are often called "clean boost" pedals instead of just "boost" pedals. Some good examples are the Xotic Effects RC Booster, MXR Micro Amp, and Z-Vex SHO.

Xotic Effects RC Booster.

 Track 40

Listen to Track 40 for a Xotic Effects RC Booster, first off and then on.

Dunlop Micro Amp.

 Track 41

Listen to Track 41 for a MXR Micro Amp, first off and then on.

Z-Vex SHO.

 **Track 42**

Listen to Track 42 for a Z-Vex SHO, first off and then on.

These examples should help you hear the primary differences in the four major types of drive pedals. But how do you search through the endless sea of pedals available today? If you address every drive style pedal with these four questions, you can compare them all on a somewhat level playing field:

1. How much drive does the pedal have?

2. What are the EQ points on the pedal?

3. How much compression does the pedal have?

4. How does the pedal respond to your hands?

Now let's look at what these questions mean:

1. The amount of drive is normally rated from next to none (Z-Vex SHO) up to as much gain as you would probably need (Electro-Harmonix Big Muff). Pedals are often classified as light, medium, or high gain by their builders and players.

2. The EQ points tell how the low, mids, and highs are altered by the pedal. The Ibanez Tube Screamer is known for having an increase in the midrange and a loss in low end while the Timmy is known for not altering your EQ much at all. The term *transparent* is often used for pedals like the Timmy.

3. The amount of compression is often not as much as you can achieve from a dedicated compression pedal, but it is present in most drive pedals. This can make the pedal feel better to the player, increase sustain, and smooth out the overall drive. Certain pedals, like the Timmy, have a diode selection switch that alters compression, along with drive.

4. The response to your hands is primarily determined by how the pedal responds to changing your volume on your guitar (or volume pedal) and when you alter your pick attack. For example, the gain from the Germanium Fuzz Face will decrease drastically if you roll back your volume and lighten up your pick attack. This is great for helping you be more dynamic without changing gear.

Finally, let's apply these four questions to some of the example pedals.

Ibanez Tube Screamer

1. Low to mid gain.

2. Increase in the mids and decrease in the lows.

3. Light to mid compression.

4. Responds to your hands fairly well.

MXR Timmy

1. Low to mid gain.

2. Very flat EQ with the ability to dial in more lows and highs. This can create somewhat of a scooped sound in the mids. But the Timmy does have a rather flat midrange.

3. Light to mid compression. The diode selection switch provides a significant change in the compression.

4. Responds to your hands very well.

Pro Co Rat

1. Mid to high gain.

2. Increase in lows and highs with little to no pronounced mids.

3. Light to mid compression. The compression increases as you turn up the distortion.

4. Responds to your hands fairly well.

Maxon SD-9

1. Low to high gain.

2. Increase in lows and highs with little midrange.

3. Light to mid compression.

4. Responds to your hands fairly well.

Dunlop Germanium Fuzz Face

1. Low to high gain.

2. Scooped in the midrange.

3. Light to mid compression.

4. Responds to your hands very well.

Dunlop Silicon Fuzz Face

1. Low to high gain.

2. Slight bump in the midrange.

3. Light to mid compression.

4. Responds to your hands very well.

Xotic Effects RC Booster

1. Low gain.

2. Very flat EQ with the ability to adjust lows and highs.

3. Light to mild compression.

4. Responds well to your hands. But since it doesn't have much gain available, it doesn't clean up very much.

Z-Vex SHO

1. Low gain.

2. Very flat EQ with some increase in the highs.

3. Mild compression.

4. Responds well to your hands. But since it doesn't have much gain available, it doesn't clean up very much.

OCTAVIA

One more style of pedal that needs to be addressed here is the *Octavia* effect. The Octavia effect is a fuzz pedal that also creates a note an octave above the note being played. The most well-known use of this effect is in the song "Purple Haze" by Jimi Hendrix.

The Octavia is a monophonic effect that is primarily used for single-note lines above the 11th fret while using the neck pickup on a Strat-style guitar. While this is not the only way to use this effect, it is the best way to hear the octave clearly.

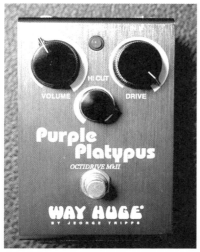

Way Huge Purple Platypus.

 Track 43

Listen to Track 43 for a Way Huge Purple Platypus played on a Strat-style guitar on the neck pickup, using single-note lines above the 11th fret, first off and then on.

 Track 44

Listen to Track 44 for a Way Huge Purple Platypus played on a Strat-style guitar on the bridge pickup, using single-note lines and chords in the lower register, first off and then on.

Gear used for recording:

Guitar: Strat-style, single-coil bridge. First Octavia clip is on the neck pickup.

Amp: 1972 Marshall Super Lead

Cabinet: Petersen 1x12, open-back

Speaker: Celestion Alnico Cream, 90-watt

Microphones: Shure SM57, Royer 121

CHAPTER 8
COMPRESSORS

Guitarists of all styles use *compression*. Some rely on the natural compression most tube amps have when they are turned up. Others get enough from the drive pedals they use. But most of today's players use compressor pedals for compression.

Primary Controls

- Input knob controls gain level of input signal.

- Output knob controls overall pedal volume.

- Ratio sets the degree of compression.

- Release knob controls how quickly your signal returns to its uncompressed level.

- Attack knob controls how quickly the compression starts.

- Dry Blend controls the balance between your compressed and non-compressed signal.

Compression is used on guitar for a multitude of reasons. But there are three primary reasons most guitarists use compression: smoothing out dynamics, increasing sustain, and as an effect. (We will address the placement of effects in Chapter 18, but the placement of a compressor pedal is so often debated among players that we will look at it here.)

The following audio clips are done with an Origin Effects Cali76 Compact Deluxe pedal. All will be done clean with the compressor off, clean with the compressor on, dirty with the compressor off, and then two passes (dirty) with the compressor on. The compressor is in front of the overdrive pedals for the first overdriven pass (diagram 1), and after for the second overdriven pass (diagram 2). If the compressor is in front of the drive pedals, it will allow for more dynamics from them. If it is placed after the drive section, it will compress the signal from the drives as well. The location of the compressor in relation to overdrives is strictly a matter of personal preference.

Diagram 1

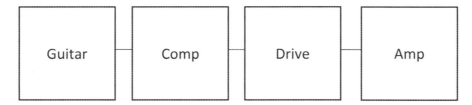

Diagram 2

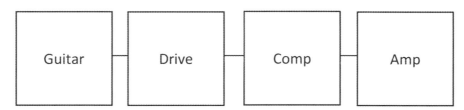

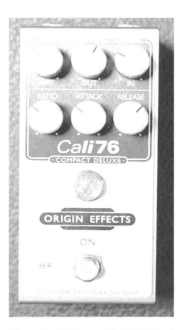

Origin Effects Cali76 Deluxe Compact Compressor.

Using Compression to Smooth Out Dynamics

Compression is often used to help smooth out the dynamics in a guitar part. This can help your part fit better in the mix of the band and keep your dynamics from stepping on other parts, especially the vocals.

 Track 45

Listen to Track 45 for a compressor set to smooth out the dynamics.

Using Compression to Increase Sustain

Compression can be used to increase the length of sustained notes. This is especially useful when playing at lower volumes, going direct, or when you are not near your amp on stage or in the studio.

 Track 46

Listen to Track 46 for a compressor set to increase sustain.

Using Compression as an Effect

Compression is also used on guitar as an audible effect. While most compression isn't designed to be heard as an obvious effect, guitarists often want it to be heard. This is often used in chicken pickin' country guitar parts.

 Track 47

Listen to Track 47 for a compressor set to use as an effect.

Using Compression for Slide

Slide guitar players often use compression to increase sustain and smooth out the dynamics while playing. While not used by all slide players (Derek Trucks is known for not using a compressor), it is still common among players (Sonny Landreth is known for using one).

 **Track 48**

Listen to Track 48 for a compressor on a slide guitar part.

Gear used for recording:

Guitar: Tele-style, single-coil bridge

Amp: 1964 Fender Vibrolux Reverb

Pedals (other than the Origin Effects Cali76 Compact Deluxe): Rockett Pedals Archer

Cabinet: Petersen 1x12, open-back

Speaker: Celestion Alnico Cream, 90-watt

Microphones: Shure SM57, Royer 121

WAH-WAH

Wah pedals were originally designed to create a sound like a person saying, "Wah-wah." Created by the Thomas Organ Company in 1966, they are expression pedals that alter the frequencies and tone of the guitar signal. Players such as Jimi Hendrix, Eric Clapton, Kirk Hammett, Tom Morello, Joe Bonamassa, and Wah-Wah Watson are only a few who are famous for using wahs. It can be heard in all styles of music from funk to metal. Trumpeter Miles Davis was even known for using a wah on his horn at times.

While there are seemingly endless ways to use these pedals, there are a few that are seen more often than most. The first is moving the wah along with the guitar part to create a more vocal line. Jimi Hendrix's recording of "Voodoo Child" is a great example of this.

Dunlop Cry Baby.

 Track 49

Listen to Track 49 for a vocal-style wah part, first off then on.

The second is moving the wah very quickly to create a "wacka-wacka" sound. This sound is evident in the "Theme from Shaft" by Isaac Hayes.

 **Track 50**

Listen to Track 50 for a "wacka-wacka" wah part, first off then on.

Finally, the use of a wah pedal as an EQ filter is very prominent. This is achieved by finding the "sweet spot" of the wah and leaving the pedal stationary. This creates an EQ filter that can range from bass heavy and muddy to thin and bright.

 **Track 51**

Listen to Track 51 for a filter-wah part, first off then on.

ENVELOPE FILTERS

Primary Controls

- Drive controls sensitivity and filter sweep range.

- Q sets the filter's bandwidth.

- Mode selects low pass, band pass, or high pass filters.

Envelope filters, also called *envelope followers* or *auto wahs*, create sounds very similar to wah pedals. But they are not normally controlled with an expression pedal. Instead, they respond to the dynamics of your picking hand. The harder you attack the strings with your picking hand, the more of the effect you will hear. This makes for a very expressive effect controlled primarily by your own dynamics.

 Track 52

Listen to Track 52 for an envelope filter, first off and then on.

Electro-Harmonix Mini Q-Tron.

TALK BOX

The *talk box effect* is designed to allow the player to talk or sing along with the guitar part, creating a unique vocal effect. This effect requires a plastic tube that is inserted in the player's mouth. As the player sings and changes the shape of their mouth, the vocal sounds are combined with the notes being played.

The Heil Talk Box was the most popular unit available for decades. This unit, originally designed by Bob Heil of Heil Sound, requires its own amp and speaker, making the setup very cumbersome for most situations. Dunlop Manufacturing Inc. purchased the design and manufactured the pedal for many years.

Due to the need for an extra amp and speaker, MXR redesigned the Talk Box to make it more compact and pedalboard-friendly. The MXR Talk Box uses your existing amp and cabinet setup, making them much easier to deal with.

Check out some of the songs listed in the back of the book for popular recorded examples of a talk box.

MXR Talk Box.

Gear used for recording:

Guitar: Strat-style, single-coil bridge

Amp: Matchless HC-30 on EF86 channel

Cabinet: Petersen 1x12, open-back

Speaker: Celestion Alnico Cream, 90-watt

Microphones: Shure SM57, Royer 121

CHAPTER 10

NOISE REDUCTION

Primary Controls

- Trigger Level knob controls the sensitivity of when the gate opens and closes.

- Noise Band Cut controls the frequency range affected by the gate.

- Hi Trigger Range is for extremely noisy rigs.

Electric guitar rigs, especially those using guitars with single-coil pickups, can be noisy. Single-coil pickups are known for creating 60-cycle hum. This noise can be enhanced with the use of effects, long cables, poor power, high gain, and amp noise. These pieces can also create their own noise along with the 60-cycle hum of single-coils.

Noise gates are the primary way that guitarists reduce noise in their rigs. Gates can be placed in multiple areas of your rig. Noise gates only reduce the noise that is created prior to their placement in the signal path. Therefore, the placement is determined by what part of your signal is creating the noise. Following are some of the primary options used by most players.

Dunlop Smart Gate.

Placing the gate immediately after the guitar will reduce the noise issue created by the guitar. The corresponding audio clip does not have any effects on since it is an example of reducing the noise created by the guitar.

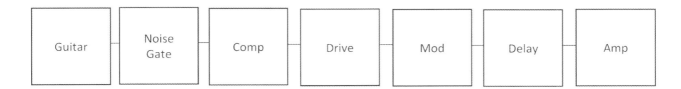

 **Track 53**

Listen to Track 53 for a clip of an MXR Smart Gate immediately after the guitar, first off and then on.

Placing the gate after the drive section of your pedalboard will reduce the noise from the guitar and your drive pedals. The corresponding audio clip adds an overdrive since it is an example of reducing the noise created by the guitar and an overdrive.

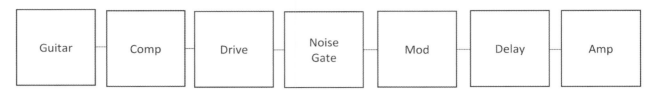

 **Track 54**

Listen to Track 54 for a clip of a MXR Smart Gate at the end of the drive section of a pedalboard, first off and then on.

Placing the gate at the end of your pedalboard will reduce the noise from all your pedals. The corresponding audio clip adds an overdrive and a tremolo effect since it is an example of reducing the noise created by the guitar, overdrive, and modulation.

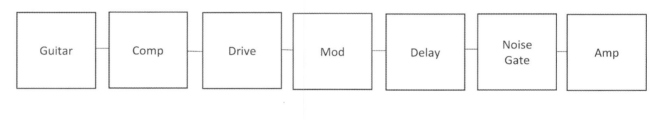

 **Track 55**

Listen to Track 55 for a clip of a MXR Smart Gate at the end of a pedalboard, first off and then on.

If your amp has an effects loop, you can place the gate in the loop. This reduces the noise from the pedals placed before the amp and prior to the gate in the loop, as well as the noise from the preamp gain of your amp. This can be particularly useful with high-gain amps. The corresponding audio clip adds an overdrive and increased gain from the amp since it is an example of reducing the noise created by the guitar, pedals, and amp.

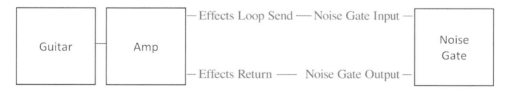

 **Track 56**

Listen to Track 56 for a clip of a MXR Smart Gate in the loop of an amp, first off and then on.

Each of these locations helps reduce the noise created by the gear that is in the signal path before the gate. But the further along in the signal path you place the gate, the more you will probably have to turn up the level of noise reduction. If you turn the level up too high, it can cause notes to be cut off too early. The key is to be mindful about your location and level. Also, you should realize that guitar rigs will always create some level of noise. The gate's primary function is to help reduce that level, not always to make it go away completely.

 Track 57

Listen to Track 57 for a clip of a MXR Smart Gate turned up high enough to cut off sustained notes and notes with low dynamics, first off and then on.

Setting a noise gate so high that it cuts off the note can also be a very useful effect. Studio great and touring guitarist David Williams would set his gate extremely high to help quickly cut off the notes he played. This meant that he had to play with an aggressive picking hand to open the gate and let the notes speak. The result is a very percussive sound found often in funk music. You can hear an example of him using this technique on Michael Jackson's song "Billie Jean."

 Track 58

Listen to Track 58 for a clip of a MXR Smart Gate turned up high enough to create a percussive guitar part, first off and then on. (This clip is done with a guitar–gate–amp signal path.)

Gear used for recording:

Guitar: Strat-style, single-coil bridge

Amp: Matchless HC-30 on EF86 channel

Pedals (other than the MXR Smart Gate): Analogman King of Tone, Strymon Mobius for tremolo

Cabinet: Petersen 1x12, open-back

Speaker: Celestion Alnico Cream, 90-watt

Microphones: Shure SM57, Royer 121

Primary controls

- Level or Volume controls the overall output volume of the pedal.

- Frequency shows the frequency you are altering.

- Sweep sets the frequency you are altering. This is only adjustable in parametric equalizers.

- "Q" sets the curve around the frequency you are altering. This can be adjusted from a large curve that alters frequencies surrounding the one labeled or with a small curve that is more precise to the selected frequency. This is only adjustable in parametric equalizers.

Equalization, or simply EQ, is a great way to sculpt and/or boost/cut your signal. Always remember that when you adjust the volume of a frequency, you are also adjusting the overall volume of the pedal. So if you boost one or more frequencies and want your overall volume to remain the same, you must turn down the level to compensate. On the other hand, if you cut one or more frequencies and you want your overall volume to remain the same, you must turn up the level to compensate. If you are both cutting and boosting frequencies, you need to use your ear to find the balance. Finally, you do not have to compensate for the changes if you don't want to. It is very common to use an EQ to cut or boost your overall level. It is all up to you and your needs.

Compensating for overall volume changes in EQ pedals is very easy if the pedal has a volume control. But, some EQ pedals, like the MXR Six-Band EQ, do not have a volume control. This means you must balance out your overall volume by evenly adjusting the frequencies you do not want to boost or cut. For example, if I want to boost 800hz by 6db, I will then evenly cut the remaining frequencies until the volume is the same with the pedal on and off. If I want to cut 800hz by 6db, I will then evenly boost the remaining frequencies until the volume is the same with the pedal on and off. This isn't always as balanced as using a volume control, but it is very effective. As always, let your ear be your guide.

There are two primary types of EQ: *graphic* and *parametric*. Let's look at both and some of their applications.

GRAPHIC EQ

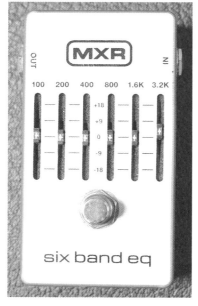

Graphic EQ gives you control of preset options, and the frequencies on a graphic EQ are labeled. For example, the MXR Six-Band EQ has frequencies set to 100hz, 200hz, 400hz, 800hz, 1.6k, and 3.2k. These frequencies and the Q are preset and cannot be changed on a graphic EQ. While this seems limiting when compared to a parametric EQ, most guitarists tend to use a graphic EQ. There are many more options for graphic EQ pedals than parametric EQ pedals, and they are much easier to use.

 Track 59

Listen to Track 59 of a MXR Six-Band EQ with pronounced mids and then scooped mids, first off and then on.

MXR Six-Band EQ.

PARAMETRIC EQ

Empress ParaEq.

Parametric EQ allows you to finetune the frequencies and the Q. For example, while the MXR Six Band EQ has settings at 800hz and 1.6k, you can tune a parametric EQ to those frequencies, or any other in between. You can also change the Q on the frequencies you are adjusting, allowing for either a more precise or loose alteration, whichever you prefer.

 Track 60

Listen to Track 60 of an Empress ParaEq with pronounced mids and then scooped mids, first off and then on.

EQ pedals have a multitude of uses for guitarists. Some of the most popular ones are to use them as a clean boost, to emphasize certain frequencies that may be otherwise lacking in your rig, to cut frequencies that are too prevalent, to cut frequencies that are causing feedback issues (most often seen on acoustic guitars), to balance out guitars that have dissimilar outputs, or to create lo-fi effects. Here are some audio clips demonstrating some of these uses of an EQ pedal.

 Track 61

Listen to Track 61 for a graphic EQ used for a clean boost, first off and then on.

 Track 62

Listen to Track 62 for a graphic EQ used to emphasize the top end, first off and then on.

 Track 63

Listen to Track 63 for a graphic EQ used to decrease the bottom end, first off and then on.

 Track 64

Listen to Track 64 for a graphic EQ used to balance the output of a bridge humbucker in a Les Paul and a bridge single-coil pickup in a Telecaster. The first pass is the Les Paul with the EQ off. The second pass is the Tele with the EQ off. The third pass is the Tele with the EQ on and with volume added to match the output of the Les Paul.

 Track 65

Listen to Track 65 for a graphic EQ used for a lo-fi effect, first off and then on.

Gear used for recording:

Guitar: Les Paul-style, humbucker bridge (except for Track 64, as listed)

Amp: 1972 Marshall Super Lead

Cabinet: Petersen 1x12, open-back

Speaker: Celestion Alnico Cream, 90-watt

Microphones: Shure SM57, Royer 121

CHAPTER 12

MODULATION EFFECTS

Modulation effects are widely used by guitarists of every genre. These effects alter the volume and/or pitch of the wave form created by the guitar. These pedals are most often placed after the drive section of a pedalboard but before the time-based effects section of a pedalboard. Let's look at some of the most popular modulation effects out there.

TREMOLO/HARMONIC TREMOLO/VIBRATO

Tremolo and *vibrato* are terms that are often used to describe three different types of effects: *tremolo*, *harmonic tremolo*, and *vibrato*. This can make speaking of them very confusing. While everyone might not agree on the terminology, we can all agree on the sound of the effects. Let's look at the three separately to help clarify the topic. (Fender uses the label "Vibrato" on amps that have tremolo and harmonic tremolo. This does help lead to the confusion in the terminology.)

Tremolo

Primary Controls

- Speed or Rate controls the time difference between the pulses in volume. This can also be controlled by tap tempo with some pedals.

- Intensity or Depth controls how much the volume is reduced with the pulse.

Tremolo is probably the most common modulation effect used by guitarists due to it being built into many popular guitar amps. It is simply a pulsing of the guitar's volume. The three most popular styles are the softer style of blackface-style Fender amps, the choppier style of Vox amps set to tremolo, and *pattern tremolo* created by outboard effects. Fender- and Vox-style tremolos stay at a consistent pulse, while pattern tremolos can be pre-programmed for a random pattern of pulses.

Strymon Flint.

 Track 66

Listen to Track 66 for a Fender-style tremolo from a Strymon Flint, first off and then on.

 **Track 67**

Listen to Track 67 for a Vox-style tremolo from a Strymon Mobius, first off and then on.

 **Track 68**

Listen to Track 68 for a pattern tremolo from a Strymon Mobius, first off and then on.

Strymon Mobius.

Harmonic Tremolo

Primary Controls

- Speed or Rate controls the time difference between the pulses in volume. This can also be controlled by tap tempo with some pedals.

- Intensity or Depth controls how much the pitch is altered with the change.

Harmonic tremolo is a volume pulse-style tremolo that includes an alteration in pitch. This is labeled "vibrato" in brownface-era Fender amps and in some Vox amps. The change in pitch is normally not drastic, but it is there in conjunction with the volume pulse. This makes for a unique sounding effect that isn't as commonly used as the standard tremolo.

 Track 69

Listen to Track 69 for a Fender-style harmonic tremolo from a Strymon Flint, first off and then on.

Vibrato

Primary Controls

- Speed or Rate controls the time difference between the pulses in pitch. This can also be controlled by tap tempo with some pedals that emulate the VB-2.

- Depth controls how much the pitch is altered with the pulse.

- Rise Time controls the time it takes to reach the maximum vibrato effect.

- Mode changes the footswitch between latched and unlatched. It can also make the pedal true bypass.

As stated before, tremolo and vibrato are often used as names for the same effect. Again, to help clarify the topic, let's look at vibrato as being separate from tremolo and harmonic tremolo.

While both styles of tremolo change the volume of the signal by using pulses, vibrato only changes the pitch of the signal. This sounds like a pitch shift effect, but it is not. It is in a class all on its own. The pitch change in vibrato pulses much like a tremolo, creating an effect like a harmonic tremolo without the changes in volume. The vibrato effect is often mistaken for a chorus.

The most popular vibrato pedal is the Boss VB-2. It was designed to emulate the vibrato effect in the Roland JC-120 amp. (Roland is the parent company of Boss.) The original VB-2 was only made from 1982–1986, making it a rare and expensive pedal. Luckily, Boss reissued the VB-2W in their Waza Craft line. The reissue is much more affordable and readily available than its vintage predecessor. The reissue offers some new features, while retaining the sound of the original VB-2.

While the vibrato effect created by the VB-2 is not heard as often as both of its tremolo counterparts, it is still widely used. Studio greats such as Michael Landau and Pat Buchanan are well known for having one on their pedalboards.

 Track 70

Listen to Track 70 from a Boss VB-2W, first off and then on.

Boss VB-2W.

CHORUS

Primary Controls

- Speed or Rate controls the time differences in the modulation. This can also be controlled by tap tempo with some pedals.

- Depth controls how intense the effect sounds.

- Mix controls the balance between the wet and dry sound.

The *chorus effect* is created by a slight delay and modulation of the guitar signal. While this is often heard on clean tones, it is also prominent on distorted tones as well. The result helps to create movement in the sound of what is being played. It is often used to enhance clean tones, widen stereo signals, and create the sound of a second guitar playing the same part.

The original chorus pedal was the Boss CE-1. The CE-1, like the VB-2, was built to create the chorus sound in the Roland JC-120 amp. As with most effects in today's market, there are a plethora of chorus pedals to choose from.

 Track 71

Listen to Track 71 for an Analogman Mini Chorus pedal, first off and then on.

Analogman Mini Chorus.

 **Track 72**

Listen to Track 72 for a Strymon Mobius set to stereo chorus, first off and then on.

 Track 73

Listen to Track 73 for a Strymon Mobius chorus used for a doubling effect, first off and then on.

PHASER

Primary Controls

- Speed controls how fast the signal goes in and out of phase. This can also be controlled by tap tempo with some pedals.

The *phaser effect* takes your guitar signal in and out of phase with itself. The MXR Phase 90 is one of the most popular phase pedals on the market. The only external control on this pedal is a speed knob. (Eddie Van Halen was known to use a Phase 90 as a solo boost in his early days with Van Halen. The vintage Phase 90 pedals have a small increase in volume when turned on.)

MXR Phase 90.

We will address the placement of effects in Chapter 18. But the placement of a phaser pedal is so often debated among players that we will look at it here. Phase is often placed either before or after the drive section of a pedalboard. This makes a difference in the overdrive tone. There is not a right or wrong placement. It is all up for you to decide what works best for you. Let's listen to both options.

 Track 74

Listen to Track 74 for a MXR Phase 90 on a clean setting, first off and then on.

 **Track 75**

Listen to Track 75 for a MXR Phase 90 set before a Rockett Archer overdrive pedal, first off and then on. (The Archer is on for both passes.)

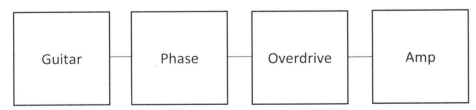

 **Track 76**

Listen to Track 76 for a MXR Phase 90 set after a Rockett Archer overdrive pedal, first off and then on. (The Archer is on for both passes.)

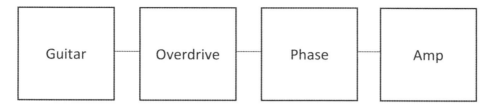

FLANGER

Primary Controls

- Manual controls the degree of phase shifting.

- Width controls the intensity of the time delay set by the speed.

- Speed controls the time delay. This can also be controlled by tap tempo with some pedals.

- Regen., or Regeneration, controls the intensity of the effect.

Flangers sound like a cross between a chorus and a phaser. It was originally created by studio engineers playing the same recording simultaneously on two different tape machines. The engineer would then place a finger on the flange of one of the tape reels and vary the amount of pressure applied. This would create a varied delay between the two tape machines, resulting in a flanging effect. Luckily, we have effects that now produce that sound for us.

 Track 77

Listen to Track 77 for a MXR Flanger, first off and then on.

MXR Flanger.

UNI-VIBE

Primary Controls

- Speed controls the time difference between the pulses. The Mobius, which is used for this recording, offers tap tempo for the speed as well.

- Depth controls how thick the pulse is. The higher you set the depth, the more dramatic the pulse.

- Volume sets the volume of the effect.

- Chorus/Vibrato switches the chorus and vibrato settings.

The *Uni-Vibe effect* is one of the many effects made famous by Jimi Hendrix. It was originally designed to create the sound of a rotary speaker, but it became its own sound. The original unit, created by Shin-Ei, included an external expression pedal to adjust the speed in real time. It also included the ability to switch between chorus and vibrato modes. The chorus mode is what most people consider the classic Uni-Vibe sound, but both are extremely usable.

 Track 78

Listen to Track 78 for a Uni-Vibe on a Strymon Mobius on the chorus setting, first off and then on.

 Track 79

Listen to Track 79 for a Uni-Vibe on a Strymon Mobius on the vibrato setting, first off and then on.

ROTARY

Primary Controls

- Drive controls the amount of overdrive.

- Fast Speed sets the speed of the effect on the fast setting.

- Slow Speed sets the speed of the effect on the slow setting.

- Microphone Distance sets the location of the microphone in relation to the two rotating speakers.

- Acceleration Time controls the amount of time it takes to change from one speed to the other.

- Horn Level controls the volume of the rotating horn in relation to the rotating drum.

Secondary Controls

- Tap Tempo sets the speed of the horn and the drum by tapping a footswitch. This will bypass the slow and fast speed settings.

Rotary effects are used to recreate the sound of an organ's Leslie speaker. Leslies have a rotating horn at the top of the cabinet and a rotating drum at the bottom of the cabinet. The player has a switch that allows them to toggle between a pre-set fast and slow setting for those speakers. The time it takes the speakers to change from one speed to the next is called the *ramp time*, or *acceleration time*.

Leslie speaker cabinet.

Leslies are run by tube amps that are mounted in the bottom of the cabinet. This, accompanied by their traditional, tube-driven organ counterpart, helps to create a beautiful overdrive when turned up. Although this is not found in all rotary cabinets, it is a part of the traditional Leslie speaker.

Some players have used actual rotary speakers to achieve this sound. Peter Frampton used a real Leslie speaker live, and in the studio, Stevie Ray Vaughan used a Fender Vibratone on his recording of "Cold Shot," and Adam Jones of Tool uses a Mesa Boogie Revolver cabinet live and in the studio.

Since owning and carrying around an extra cabinet is not practical for most players, there are pedals designed to emulate the sound. Most rotary effects allow the player to adjust the level of the horn and the drum independently, as well as the ramp time. Some rotary effects also include a tap tempo option. This allows the player to set the speed of both speaker simulations in time with the music being played. While this is not consistent with a traditional Leslie sound, it is very useful. Let's listen to a couple of pedal emulations of a rotary cabinet.

 Track 80

Listen to Track 80 for a rotary effect from a Strymon Mobius ramping between a slow and fast setting, first off and then on.

 Track 81

Listen to Track 81 for a rotary effect from a Strymon Mobius using a tap tempo option, first off and then on.

RING MODULATION

Primary Controls

- Speed controls how fast the sound is modulated. This can also be controlled by tap tempo with some pedals.

- Depth controls the thickness of the modulation.

- Pitch sets the note created.

- Mix controls the balance between the wet and dry sound.

Ring modulation effects can go from subtle to drastic. The sonic result can range from a tremolo effect to a synth-like sound that doesn't even resemble the notes being played. They are often used for "out" sounding effects by dialing the controls, especially the mix, to extreme settings. But they can also be used for a layering type of effect to give another dimension to your sound.

The audio clip here is done with a Strymon Mobius pedal. While this pedal does not have a dedicated ring-mod setting, it does have the option. If you use the Quadrature effect with the mode set to AM, you can achieve a great ring-mod sound.

 **Track 82**

Listen to Track 82 for a Strymon Mobius set to a ring-mod effect, first off and then on.

Gear used for recording:

Guitar: Strat-style, single-coil neck

Amp: 1964 Fender Vibrolux Reverb, Stereo Chorus has '59 Fender Bassman RI

Cabinet: Petersen 1x12, open-back

Speaker: Celestion Alnico Cream, 90-watt

Microphones: Shure SM57, Royer 121, Stereo Chorus uses two SM57s

CHAPTER 13

DELAY

Primary Controls

- Delay controls the length of time of your delay. This is also controlled by the tap tempo footswitch on pedals with that option.

- Repeats or Feedback controls the number of times the delayed part is repeated. This can be turned up on many delay pedals to make them self-oscillate and start to feed back.

- Mix controls the balance between the dry signal and the delayed signal.

- Level controls the overall volume of the pedal.

Delay pedals are seen in almost every guitar player's rig, regardless of style. They are not only fun to play, but they add a depth to a part that is often sorely missed when not present. With the plethora of delay options out there, how do you find what you need? Here is a list of criteria that is useful when picking a delay pedal:

1. Do you want *analog* or *digital*? (Analog includes any delay that is not digital.)

2. How much delay time do you need?

3. Do you want tap tempo?

4. Do you want presets?

5. Do you need it to work in an effects loop?

Now let's look at what these questions mean:

1. Most players want an analog delay, or at least a digital pedal that emulates the sound of an analog delay. Analog will generally give you a warmer sound than digital, but it can be more limited in terms of longer delay times, tap tempo, and presets. Digital delays often offer emulations of other sounds including analog, tape, ping-pong, modulation, reverse, and filter.

2. The most common maximum delay times for an analog pedal are 300 or 600 milliseconds, with some longer options available. Half of one second is equal to 500 milliseconds. Digital pedals can have delay times several seconds long.

3. Tap tempo is the option to set the delay time by tapping on a secondary footswitch. This allows your delays to quickly and easily be in time with the rest of the music being played. Tap tempo is now available in many analog delay pedals and in most digital ones. This makes it much easier to set the delay in time with the rest of the music, especially in a live setting.

   Tap tempo can often be set to different rhythmic divisions. This allows you to tap a quarter note and have the delay set to divisions such as a quarter note, dotted-eighth note, eighth-note triplet, etc. This can be very useful since tapping some of these divisions can prove to be very difficult.

4. Presets in delay pedals can be extremely useful. They allow you to have multiple delay sounds available with the tap of a button. This is great for having a rhythm sound and a lead sound or having a different sound for different songs. Analog delay pedals with presets are extremely rare, while digital ones are readily available from multiple companies.

5. While not all amps have effects loops, many do. They are primarily found in, but not limited to, high-gain and multi-channel amps. Most loops are set to a level of -10 (instrument level) and will work with almost every pedal available. Some amps do have a level of +4 (line level) and will only work with pedals that can accept +4.

Now that we know the criteria to evaluate, let's discuss some options. Following is a short list of popular delay pedals that offer the previously mentioned options. (All the audio clips for this chapter are accompanied by a drum loop to show the function of tap tempo.)

ANALOG DELAY WITHOUT TAP TEMPO

Analog delays without tap tempo are the most basic type of delay commonly used by guitarists. They are often revered for their warm sound and ease of use. It is very difficult to set them in time with the music since they do not have tap tempo.

The MXR Carbon Copy Mini is a great example of an analog delay without tap tempo. It has a nice, warm sound and is very easy to use. The modulation switch allows you to add modulation to the repeats. This is explained in the next example.

 Track 83

Listen to Track 83 for a MXR Carbon Copy Mini, first off and then on.

MXR Carbon Copy Mini.

The Electro-Harmonix Deluxe Memory Man is another example of an analog delay without tap tempo. We will discuss this pedal here as well since it is one of the most popular delay pedals of all time. (There are tap tempo versions of the Memory Man, but they sound different.)

Secondary Controls

- Chorus/Vibrato switches between chorus and vibrato for the modulation.

- Depth controls how thick the modulation sounds.

The Electro-Harmonix Deluxe Memory Man is unique because it is a modulated delay. This means that it adds chorus or vibrato to the delayed signal. This differs from adding a separate chorus or vibrato to your signal because the modulation is only on your delayed notes and not on your dry signal. This pedal is also often used for the self-oscillating effect.

The Memory Man is known for creating a unique overdriven sound when the level is turned up. While this can pose an issue with your volume when you turn the pedal on or off, it can still be very useful. Players often use this overdriven sound in the studio since they don't have to worry about changes in volume as much.

 Track 84

Listen to Track 84 for an Electro-Harmonix Deluxe Memory Man set to a few repeats with the modulation on, first off and then on.

 Track 85

Listen to Track 85 for an Electro-Harmonix Memory Man set to enough repeats to let the pedal self-oscillate, first off and then on.

 Track 86

Listen to Track 86 for an Electro-Harmonix Memory Man set to an overdriven sound, first off and then on.

Electro-Harmonix Deluxe Memory Man.

ANALOG DELAY WITH TAP TEMPO

MXR's Carbon Copy Deluxe is an expanded version of their Carbon Copy and Carbon Copy Mini. This pedal includes a longer delay time, more control of the modulation, tap tempo, different tap divisions, an expression pedal option, and a bright setting for the tone of the repeats.

The Carbon Copy Deluxe does allow you to switch between two settings, technically making it an analog delay with a preset. While this makes the pedal extremely versatile, some players might want more than two options when using presets.

 Track 87

Listen to Track 87 of a MXR Carbon Copy Deluxe, first off then on with tap tempo. (Pay attention to how the delays are in time with the drum loop.)

MXR Carbon Copy Deluxe.

DIGITAL DELAY WITH TAP TEMPO

The Dunlop EP103 Echoplex delay pedal is a digital delay with the option of an external tap tempo switch. The use of the tap tempo option on this pedal extends the delay time to a full four seconds, making it great for long delays. It is designed to recreate the sound of the desirable and expensive vintage tape delays.

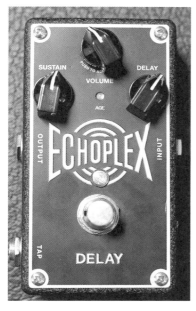

Dunlop EP103 Echoplex.

Secondary Controls

- Tape Age is controlled by pressing down the volume control. This helps recreate the characteristics of older tape being used in tape delays.

 Track 88

Listen to Track 88 of a Dunlop EP103 Echoplex first off and then on with tap tempo. (The tape age is turned off.)

ANALOG DELAY WITH TAP TEMPO AND PRESETS

Analogman's ARDX20 coupled with the Amaze1 controller is one of the few analog delays on the market that allows tap tempo and multiple presets. Analogman Mike Piera is well known as one of the top manufacturers of boutique pedals. The ARDX20 coupled with the Amaze1 controller allows tap tempo, multiple presets, modulation for the delays, an effects loop, and the warm sound of analog. Even though it is not seen as often as the other delays listed in this chapter, it is still considered one of the top units on the market.

Analogman ARDX20 with Amaze1 controller.

Secondary Controls

- The effects loop allows you to add an effect to the repeats. This acts like the modulation on a modulated delay like the Memory Man Deluxe. The effect(s) you place in the loop will only be on the repeats.

 Track 89

Listen to Track 89 of an Analogman ARDX20 with the Amaze1 controller, first off and then on with an octave in the loop.

DIGITAL DELAY WITH TAP TEMPO AND PRESETS

Many current delay pedals offer models of multiple types of classic and modern delays. The Strymon TimeLine is a great example of a pedal that offers several models based on other effects. Here are some audio examples using the TimeLine:

 Track 90

Listen to Track 90 for a Strymon TimeLine model of a modulated delay, first off and then on. (This is designed to emulate a modulated delay like the Electro-Harmonix Deluxe Memory Man.)

 Track 91

Listen to Track 91 for a Strymon TimeLine model of an analog delay, first off and then on. (This is designed to emulate an analog delay pedal like the MXR Carbon Copy.)

 Track 92

Listen to Track 92 for a Strymon TimeLine model of a tape delay, first off and then on. (This is designed to emulate an actual tape delay, such as an Echoplex.)

 Track 93

Listen to Track 93 for a Strymon TimeLine model of a stereo delay, first off and then on. (This gives you stereo delays, allowing repeats on each side to be split.)

 Track 94

Listen to Track 94 for a Strymon TimeLine model of a lo-fi delay, first off and then on. (This is designed to emulate delays that cannot accurately recreate the dry signal.)

 Track 95

Listen to Track 95 for a Strymon TimeLine model of a ducked delay, *first off and then on. Ducked delays are very useful, especially when soloing. They decrease the volume of the delayed signal while you are still playing on top of the delayed notes. The delayed signal becomes louder when you stop playing, making your overall sound clearer.*

DELAYS IN EFFECTS LOOPS

Since delays are often used in effects loops, let's discuss this scenario here. (The information on effects loop levels applies to all pedals placed in a loop, not just delays.)

Delays can sound cleaner and more controlled when used in the effects loop of an amp. But you must make sure that your delay is compatible with the effects loop in your amp. Most amps are -10, or *instrument level*, but some are set to +4, or *line level*. You need to make sure that the loop and delay you are using will accept the same level. You can check the level of both by checking with the manufacturers.

Many pedals, like the Strymon TimeLine, can accept both levels without changing any settings. Pedals like the Analogman ARDX20 are only designed to work well in instrument level loops. Pedals like this are not designed to be placed in a line level loop, only one set to instrument level. They need to be placed in front of the amp if the loop cannot be set to instrument level.

 Track 96

Listen to Track 96 of an Analogman ARDX20 in front of a VHT amp, then in the line level effects loop of the amp. (The settings on the pedal do not change. Notice how the delays change due to the level of the effects loop.)

Effects loops are extremely useful, especially when using multi-channel amps. If you run your delay into the front of a multi-channel amp the characteristics of the delay change when you change from a clean to distorted tone. The delay will remain much more consistent with channel switching when run in the effects loop.

 Track 97

Listen to Track 97 of an Strymon TimeLine in the front of a multi-channel VHT amp, first clean and then dirty. (The preset on the TimeLine is the same for both passes. Notice how the delays change when the amp channels are changed.)

Strymon TimeLine.

 Track 98

Listen to Track 98 of a Strymon TimeLine in the effects loop of a multi-channel VHT amp, first clean and then dirty. (The preset on the TimeLine is the same as used on the previous clip. Notice how the delay is more consistent with channel changes when placed in the effects loop.)

LOOPERS

Looper pedals allow the guitarist to record the parts being played and then play them back just like recording them in a studio. They are like delays in that they repeat what is being played, but they continue to play the part(s) until turned off. Many modern digital delays offer a looper on them, but there are dedicated looper pedals as well. Players like Phil Keaggy and Ed Sheeran are well known for using loopers live to create multiple parts and build their songs on their own.

Loopers are great practice tools as well. Recording a part and then working on additional parts or solos are a great way to utilize a looper.

Check out Chad Johnson's *Looper Pedal Songbook* and *Looper Pedal Guitar Lessons* (both from Hal Leonard) if you would like to explore the use of looper pedals.

Gear used for recording:

Guitar: Strat-style, single-coil neck

Amp: 1964 Fender Vibrolux Reverb, stereo delay has '59 Fender Bassman RI, VHT Pitbull CLX for the effects loop example

Cabinet: Petersen 1x12, open-back

Speaker: Celestion Alnico Cream, 90-watt

Microphones: Shure SM57, Royer 121, stereo uses two SM57s

Primary Controls

- Decay controls the amount of time it takes for the reverb to die off.

- Pre-Delay controls the amount of time between the notes being played and when the reverb starts.

- Mix controls the balance of wet to dry signal.

- Tone controls the tone of the reverb, not your dry signal.

- Modulation adds modulation to the reverb, not your dry signal.

Reverb is all around us in our daily lives. It is created naturally by sound reflecting on surrounding surfaces. These reflections are too short to be interpreted as delay and are heard as reverb. The size of the space and the number of reflections alter the amount of reverb heard. For example, the reverb you hear in your bedroom is drastically different than what you hear in an arena.

Reverb was originally created for guitar to add space and depth to the sound, but it has changed drastically over the years. Since reverb is primarily used to create space, the recordings for this chapter will be done using a Universal Audio OX going direct instead of live microphones in a room. This will let us focus on the reverb we create, not what would be created by the natural space. The OX is set to be completely dry.

All the reverb sounds for this chapter, except the example of spring reverb in the Fender Vibrolux Reverb, will be done with a Strymon Big Sky Reverb pedal. While some of the controls listed are specific to this pedal, the overall application can be applied to all reverbs. Let's look at a few options for reverb.

Strymon Big Sky.

SPRING REVERB

Secondary Controls

- Low End controls the level of the bass frequencies in your wet sound.

- Dwell controls the amount of drive in the preamp circuit. This helps to emulate the preamp circuit in traditional spring reverbs.

- Number of Springs controls how many springs are being emulated. The more springs you use, the more complex the reverb.

Reverb is the most common effect found in guitar amps. The most common reverb in amps is *spring reverb*. This effect is created by the guitar signal being sent to a metal box with springs stretched out inside. The signal then causes the springs to vibrate, creating the reverb. It is very common for reverb pedals to have a model based on this sound.

Fender Vibrolux Reverb.

You will also see independent *spring reverb tanks*. They are a stand-alone spring reverb designed to create the effect naturally instead of being modeled in a pedal. Brian Setzer is one guitarist well known for using spring reverb tanks for his tone.

 Track 99

Listen to Track 99 for a spring reverb in a Fender Vibrolux Reverb, first off and then on. (This is what an actual spring reverb sounds like.)

 Track 100

Listen to Track 100 for a Strymon Big Sky Reverb set to "spring," first off and then on.

Reverb effects are also used to recreate the sound of being in a specific space. This is often referred to as *hall* or *room*.

HALL REVERB

Secondary Controls

- Low End controls the level of the bass frequencies in your wet sound.

- Mid controls the level of the midrange frequencies in your wet sound.

- Size changes the physical size of the hall you are emulating. The larger the hall, the more reverb you have available.

A hall reverb is designed to emulate the sound of being in an actual concert hall. Think about how it sounds to hear a concert in a concert hall or arena. The reflections off the walls, floor, ceiling, and objects in the hall create a natural reverb. The bigger the hall, the more reflections you will have, creating more reverb. Digital reverbs emulate that sound, allowing us to create the feeling of being in a concert hall, no matter where we are.

 Track 101

Listen to Track 101 for a Strymon Big Sky Reverb set to "hall," first off and then on.

ROOM REVERB

Secondary Controls

- Low End controls the level of the bass frequencies in your wet sound.

- Size selects between studio and club settings. The studio is more controlled, while the club is much livelier.

- Diffusion controls the early reflections of your reverb. This can help to create a fuller attack of the reverb.

A room reverb is designed to emulate the sound of being in a space smaller than a concert hall. The emulation of a club or professional recording studio are two popular options used in digital room models. The club setting will give you more of a live sound overall, since most clubs are not treated with any sound dampening.

 Track 102

Listen to Track 102 for a Strymon Big Sky Reverb set to "room" on the club setting, first off and then on.

The studio setting emulates more of a controlled environment. This allows you to recreate the sound of being in a professional recording studio. This sound tends to be more refined than the club setting.

 Track 103

Listen to Track 103 for a Strymon Big Sky Reverb set to "room" on the studio setting, first off and then on.

PLATE REVERB

Secondary Controls

- Low End controls the level of the bass frequencies in your wet sound.

- Size changes the physical size of the plate you are emulating. The larger the plate, the more reverb you can dial in.

Plate reverb is a common effect used in many high-end studios. The effect is created by sending the signal across a thin plate of metal that is enclosed in a case. The vibration of the metal plate creates the effect, much like the vibrating of springs in a spring reverb. The result is like a room reverb but has its own unique tone. Plates are large and expensive, making them unavailable to most of us. Luckily, there are some great options for models of plate reverbs.

 Track 104

Listen to Track 104 for a Strymon Big Sky Reverb set to "plate," first off and then on.

As a guitar effect, reverb has evolved past just the recreation of space. There are many options out now that take the traditional idea of reverb to new and interesting places. They are often used to create ambience in parts far beyond their previous counterparts. Let's look at a couple of popular examples.

SHIMMER REVERB

Secondary Controls

- Shift 1 selects the first pitch shifted interval.

- Shift 2 selects the second pitch shifted interval.

- Amount controls the mix of the pitch shifted frequencies within the reverb.

- Mode adjusts if/how pitch shifted frequencies are regenerated.

- Low End controls the level of the bass frequencies in your wet sound.

Shimmer reverb adds pitch shifting to the wet signal only. This is different from running a guitar into a pitch shifter and then into reverb. If you use the two effects independently, the pitch shift will be on the dry signal of the guitar and the reverb will be added to that signal. With a shimmer reverb, only the signal of the reverb has pitch shifting. The dry signal does not have any pitch shifting from the shimmer reverb effect.

 Track 105

Listen to Track 105 for a Strymon Big Sky Reverb set to "shimmer," first off and then on.

SWELL REVERB

Secondary Controls

- Low End controls the level of the bass frequencies in your wet sound.

- Rise Time controls the amount of time of the swelled signal.

Swell reverb can be set in two modes. First, it can bring the reverb into the dry signal as you are playing. This is like having an expression pedal on your reverb and blending it in with your playing. Second, it can bring the dry signal into the reverb. This is like having your reverb on and using an expression pedal to blend in your dry signal. Swell reverb is great for ambient guitar tones.

 Track 106

Listen to Track 106 for a Strymon Big Sky Reverb set to "swell" with the reverb swelling into the dry signal, first off and then on.

 Track 107

Listen to Track 107 for a Strymon Big Sky Reverb set to "swell" with the dry signal swelling into the reverb, first off and then on.

Gear used for recording:

Guitar: Strat-style, single-coil neck

Amp: 1964 Fender Vibrolux Reverb

Cabinet: Universal Audio OX V-ux 2x10

Microphones: Universal Audio SM57, Royer 121

CHAPTER 15
PITCH SHIFTERS

Primary Controls

- Output controls the overall volume of the pedal.

- Mix controls the balance between the wet and dry signal.

- Pitch controls what pitch or pitches are being added to your signal.

Pitch effects are used to create notes other than the ones you are playing. There are five characteristics of pitch effects that we are going to look at.

MONOPHONIC PITCH SHIFTERS

These effects are designed to only do one note at a time. They are great for processing single lines, but they do not do well on chords. The Digitech Whammy 5 set to classic mode is an example of a monophonic pitch pedal.

 Track 108

Listen to Track 108 for a Digitech Whammy 5 set to "classic" mode with an octave up on the "harmony" mode, first off and then on.

Digitech Whammy.

POLYPHONIC PITCH SHIFTERS

These effects are designed to pitch shift more than one note at a time. They are great for creating 12-string sounds on a 6-string (the top two strings will be an octave up instead of doubled, but it can be OK for certain situations), baritone sounds on standard tuned guitar, or adding harmony whenever you are playing more than one note. The Digitech Whammy 5 set to chords mode is an example of a polyphonic pitch shifter pedal.

 Track 109

Listen to Track 109 for a Digitech Whammy 5 set to "chords" mode with an octave up on the "harmony" mode, first off and then on.

FIXED PITCH SHIFTERS

These effects give you a specific interval that does not change in relation to the key you are playing in. While this is fine with octaves, it can be an issue with intervals such as a perfect 4th. For example, the notes in the key of C major are C–D–E–F–G–A–B–C. If you set a fixed pitch shifter to a perfect 4th and play the C major scale everything will stay within the key until you play an F. This will result in a B♭ (perfect 4th) instead of a B natural (augmented 4th). While this can be what you are looking for, keep in mind that it will take you out of the key. The Electro-Harmonix Pitch Fork is an example of a fixed pitch shifter pedal.

 Track 110

Listen to Track 110 for a Pitch Fork set with the harmony to a perfect 4th, first off and then on. (I pause on the F note so you can clearly hear the B♭.)

Pitch Fork pitch shifter.

INTELLIGENT PITCH SHIFTERS

Secondary Controls

- Key sets notes played by the effect to be in that particular key.

- Major/Minor changes the notes from the key control to be major or minor.

Intelligent pitch shifters allow you to assign a key to what you are playing. This will compensate for the changing of the assigned interval within the assigned key. For example, if you play the same line we played in the previous example, the harmony for the F note with be a B♮ instead of a B♭. This is a major advantage when you consider the only interval that is consistent throughout the major scale is the octave. The Electro-Harmonix Intelligent Harmony Machine is an example of an intelligent pitch shifter pedal.

Intelligent Harmony Machine.

 Track 111

Listen to Track 111 for an Intelligent Harmony Machine set to a perfect 4th, first off and then on. (I pause on the F note so you can clearly hear the B♮.)

PITCH SHIFTERS WITH EXPRESSION CONTROL

Secondary Control

- Expression Control allows the pitch to be manipulated in real time.

Pitch shifters with expression control let you manipulate the changing of the pitch in real time. For example, if you set one of these effects to an octave up you can slide the pitch up to the octave as fast or slow as you would like. This sound is similar to using a slide on your guitar instead of just placing your fingers on the fretboard. Dimebag Darrell of Pantera and Tom Morello of Rage Against the Machine/Audioslave are well known for using this effect.

The Digitech Whammy pedal is probably the most famous of these types of pedals. The Whammy pedal was groundbreaking when it was first released. Now there are several versions of the pedal, along with multiple pedals from other manufacturers that create the same style of effect. Some of these pedals, such as the Whammy 5, do not have a mix option. In the harmony setting, you will hear a preset mix of your original note(s) and the harmony, but in the Whammy mode, you will only hear the harmony. Other pedals, such as the Electro-Harmonix Pitch Fork, do have a mix option. This allows you to mix the original note(s) and the harmony however you desire.

 Track 112

Listen to Track 112 for a Digitech Whammy 5 with an octave up in the "whammy" mode, first off and then on.

Pitch effects have many uses. Let's look at a few.

1. They can create harmony with what is already being played.

   This allows playing multiple parts or added harmony much easier. You must adjust the mix to less than 100% wet to create this effect. We can set an octave down on an Electro-Harmonix POG 2 to easily hear this.

 Track 113

Listen to Track 113 for a POG 2 set to an octave down and mix at 50% wet for a harmony line, first off and then on.

Electro-Harmonix POG 2.

2. They can create a different line than what is being played.

   This is obtained by setting the mix to 100% wet, thereby not allowing what you are actually playing to be heard. Again, let's set the POG 2 to one octave down.

 Track 114

Listen to Track 114 for a POG 2 set to an octave down and mix 100% wet, first off and then on.

3. They can be used to simulate a capo, or to create the sound of a tuned-down guitar.

This is done the same way as Track 114, but there are specific pedals designed to do this.

The Digitech Drop is designed specifically for this effect. The Drop is a polyphonic pitch shifter that shifts your signal down as far as seven semitones or one octave. There is also an octave setting that blends your original signal for a harmony option. This effect is very useful for quickly transposing parts on a gig. While this use of the effect is sometimes done in the studio, it is most often used in live situations.

Pedals like the Drop are very useful for transposing your guitar parts down on live gigs. The lick in the next example is very similar to a well-known southern rock song. This lick incorporates open strings, making it difficult to correctly play it in a different key. As you can hear, the Drop does a good job of transposing down to make things easier for you.

Digitech Drop.

 **Track 115**

Listen to Track 115 for a Digitech Drop tuned down three semitones, first off and then on.

4. They can be used to create a pitch that is slightly out of tune.

This requires an effect that can dial up detuning in cents instead of fixed intervals. While being slightly out of tune doesn't sound like a good idea, it can be very useful. Guitarists use this trick to create the sound of multiple guitars playing the same part. Since players play differently, and it is extremely difficult to get two guitars perfectly in tune with each other, a very slight pitch shift helps to emulate that.

 Track 116

Listen to Track 116 for a Pitch Fork set to a doubling effect, first off and then on.

The main thing to pay attention to when using pitch shifting is the interval(s) you are using and the mix knob. If you keep those two things in mind, you can come up with endless ideas that utilize pitch shifting effects.

Gear used for recording:

Guitar: Tele-style, single-coil neck

Amp: 1972 Marshall Super Lead

Cabinet: Petersen 1x12, open-back

Speaker: Celestion Alnico Cream, 90-watt

Microphones: Shure SM57, Royer 121

CHAPTER 16
OTHER EFFECTS

While most effects can be classified under the previous chapters, some cannot. Some are designed for control, and some create sounds that are extremely unique. Since it would be impossible to address all the creations in the market today, let's look at how to approach them.

VOLUME PEDALS

Volume pedals are designed to act like the volume knob on your guitar. They are very useful, considering it can be difficult to adjust the volume knob on your guitar when playing. The placement of them is very important and is addressed in Chapter 18.

EXPRESSION PEDALS

Expression pedals often resemble volume pedals in their design. The Volume X series from Dunlop can be used as an expression or volume pedal. Expression pedals are designed to allow you to change a parameter of an effect with your foot instead of having to reach down and turn a knob. This is extremely useful on live gigs. Not all pedals allow the use of expression pedals, so make sure it is an option on the effect you are using.

Some common uses of expression pedals are altering repeats on a delay, increasing the mix of an effect, changing the depth of an effect, or changing the speed of an effect when not using tap tempo. Most modelers have extensive options with the use of expression pedals. You can often program one movement of an expression pedal to change multiple parameters in real time.

TRUE BYPASS LOOPERS

True bypass loopers can be a single loop or multiple loops. Single loops are often used to bypass an effect that alters your tone while turned off. Multiple loops can have each pedal from your board in its own loop. This allows you to be able to turn the signal to your pedals on and off without reaching over other pedals with your foot. Multiple loops are most often seen on large touring and studio boards.

OVERALL SOUND CHANGES

Most pedals that do not have the basic characteristics of those we have discussed in previous chapters still act similarly. If they change the basic sound of your guitar, try placing them towards the front of your signal path. Those that are based around crazy modulations will probably work best in the middle of the chain, while those that are time-based are often placed towards the end.

Some non-traditional pedals combine two or more effects, like fuzz and tremolo, that are normally placed in different sections of your signal path. Since these effects are normally placed in different sections of the pedalboard, try addressing what you are using as the most prominent sound and start there. So if you are treating it like a fuzz with a tremolo, try placing it in the drive section of your signal path. If you are using the pedal like a tremolo with some fuzz, try placing it in the modulation section of your board.

The placement and use of non-traditional effects is completely up to you. They can be fun noise makers that spark creativity, or they can become the basis of your tone. At one point, the fuzz pedal was considered non-traditional, and now it is one of the necessities for most players.

Always keep in mind how your signal path works. When more than one pedal is turned on in your chain, pedals placed earlier in the chain can alter the tone of any pedals that follow. This should help you start with your experimentation.

CHAPTER 17

BUFFERED-BYPASS, TRUE-BYPASS, AND BUFFER PEDALS

All pedals have two options when they are turned off: *buffered bypass* or *true bypass*. The simplest way to think about these two options is as follows.

1. Buffered Bypass

Buffered-bypass pedals send your signal through the pedal's internal buffer when the pedal is turned off. The buffer will alter your signal, even if it is very slight or inaudible to you.

2. True Bypass

True-bypass pedals do not have a buffer and essentially connect the input of the pedal to the output of the pedal when turned off. This sounds like a superior design, but it does have its flaws.

Both bypass options have their place in the pedal world. There is not a definite answer of one design being better than the other, only what is better for the pedal and application.

Boss DD-500.

For example, most people set delay pedals to buffered bypass instead of true bypass. The buffered option allows the delays to trail after the pedal has been turned off. This results in the continuation of your delay and normally sounds more natural. The true-bypass option turns the delay trails off when the pedal is off. This can sound abrupt to some people. The choice is completely personal preference. Therefore, pedals like the Boss DD-500 can be set to buffered bypass or true bypass.

 Track 117

Listen to Track 117 for a Boss DD-500 delay set to buffered bypass and turned off while repeats are still trailing.

 Track 118

Listen to Track 118 for a Boss DD-500 delay set to true bypass and turned off while repeats are still trailing.

Players with several pedals on their board will often experience some loss in signal, especially in the top end. You can often hear this by listening to your guitar straight into your amp, then listening to it with the pedalboard in the signal chain. Even with all your pedals turned off, you will probably hear a change in tone.

This is most common when most or all pedals being used are true bypass. A common way to make up for this signal loss is to add a high-quality, stand-alone buffer at the beginning or end of the pedalboard.

 Track 119

Listen to Track 119 for a pedalboard first without a buffer, then with a MXR CAE Buffer at the beginning of the board (Diagram 1), then with the MXR buffer at the end of the board (Diagram 2).

As you can hear, using the buffer at the end of the board has the biggest change to the sound. The buffer placed at the beginning of the board changes the feel of the rig more than the volume. Sadly, this can only be felt by the player, not heard. The level on the buffer is at its maximum setting for both audio clips to emphasize the differences.

Diagram 1

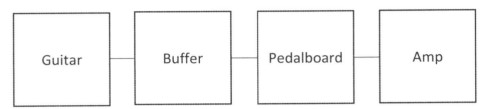

Diagram 2

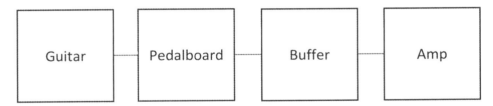

MXR CAE Buffer.

Pedalboard in use.

Gear used for recording:

Guitar: Gibson ES-335, bridge pickup

Amp: 1972 Marshall Super Lead

Cabinet: Petersen 1x12, open-back

Speaker: Celestion Alnico Cream, 90-watt

Microphones: Shure SM57, Royer 121

CHAPTER 18

PLACING EFFECTS IN YOUR RIG

The effects you choose for your rig is a very personal choice that constantly evolves for most of us. Whether you use pedals, rack gear, or modelers, the principals of signal flow remain the same. For our purposes here, we will deal with pedals.

Very few guitar players buy a handful of pedals, build a board, and then leave that setup for years to come. Our tastes in tone, the gigs we play, and what is available on the market change. So our needs and desires for pedals change. Also, pedals are lots of fun, so experiment and enjoy!

The order of your effects has a drastic impact on your tone. The interaction of pedals can change with respect to where they are in the signal chain. As we have seen in prior chapters, the placement of effects such as compressors, phasers, and noise gates are very subjective. The truth is that the order you place your effects in is completely up to you, the player.

While the placement of effects is up to the player, there is a standard order in which most players run their effects. The most popular signal flow is drive section–modulation section–time-based section. Following are a few diagrams of popular signal flows for pedalboards.

This first signal flow has the compressor before the drives, allowing the drives to be more dynamic. The boost is after the drives, allowing an increase in volume with or without the drives being on. By having the boost after the drives, you can increase your volume without pushing the drive pedals harder. The volume pedal is after the drives, allowing the gain of the drives to stay the same no matter the level of the volume pedal. The modulation and time effects are placed at the end of the signal path for the cleanest overall sound.

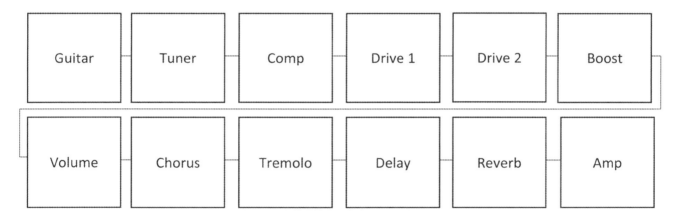

The second signal flow (on the next page) is very similar to the first one, but the volume and boost pedals are in front of the drive section. Placing the volume before the drives results in a reduction in gain from the drive pedals as the volume on the pedal is reduced. The advantage to this setup is that you can reduce the drive created by your pedals by turning down your volume pedal. Placing the boost before the overdrives can push them into having more gain when the boost and one or both drives are on.

The tremolo/reverb effect is listed as a single slot due to popular pedals like the Strymon Flint that combine the two effects into one pedal.

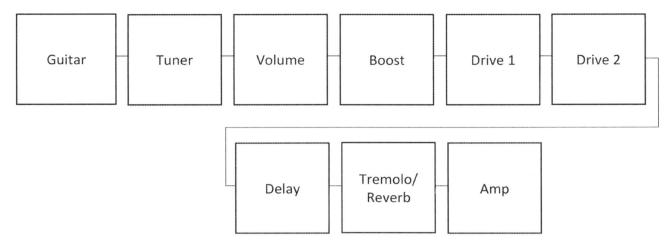

The third signal flow has the fuzz before everything and an EQ in place of a boost. Most fuzz pedals, especially vintage-style ones, do not like to see any other pedals before them. As with any effect placed in front of a tuner, make sure they are turned off when tuning your guitar.

The EQ is placed after the drive so it can be used to boost the signal just like the boost pedal in the first example. It can also be placed in front of the drive, like the second example. They can act just like a boost pedal, or they can be used to sculpt the overall tone of your rig.

The wah pedal is also in the first part of the signal path. Wahs and envelope filters are normally at the very front of the signal path, with only fuzz pedals and tuners preceding them.

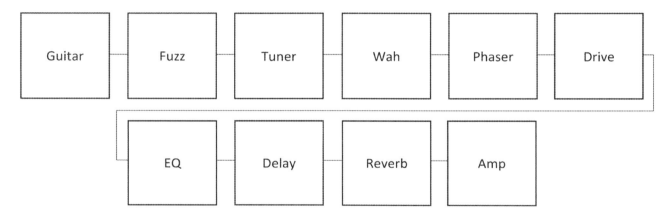

The fourth and final signal flow adds a pitch pedal to the signal path. Pitch pedals tend to track better when placed before other effects. The compressor is placed after the pitch to help level out the signal when the pitch effect is added.

Placing your delay near the end of your signal path is considered standard. This allows for a cleaner and more consistent sound from your delay when you combine it with a drive. Placing the delay before the drive results in less defined delay tones and a change in the repeats. As with everything, the choice is all yours.

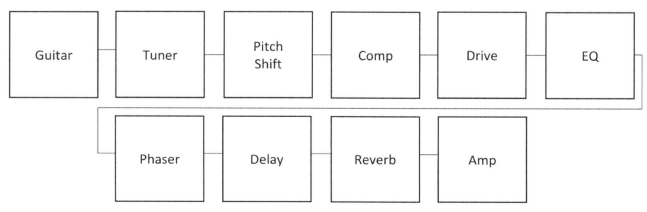

 **Track 120**

Listen to Track 120 for a Rockett Archer into a Strymon TimeLine. (The first pass is clean, the second adds the delay, and the third has delay and overdrive.)

 **Track 121**

Listen to Track 121 for a Strymon TimeLine into a Rockett Archer. (The first pass is clean, the second adds the delay, and the third has delay and overdrive. The settings are the same as the previous clip.)

STACKING PEDALS

The term *stacking pedals* refers to turning on more than one pedal at the same time. Having more than one pedal on at the same time not only gives you the sounds of those effects, but it also creates a reaction between them. While stacking some pedals gives you little more than the sound of both effects, some combinations bring on an entirely new tone.

Stacking Drives

It is common to stack pedals in the drive section. Keep in mind that stacking drive pedals will increase your noise level as well. Here are a few common ways to stack drives.

A common way to stack drive style pedals is by using a fuzz, boost, or overdrive for your rhythm sound and adding a boost pedal for solos. Stacking these styles of pedals will give you more volume, gain, and sustain than your rhythm sound. Doing this is especially beneficial if you do not have someone running sound that knows your set. Boosting your signal for solos can let you be heard even if the sound person doesn't turn up your volume. Be sure to turn off your boost after you solo so you don't drown out everyone else.

Stacking overdrives and/or distortions is also very common. Players will often use a low gain drive and a medium gain drive on their boards to cover most tones needed for a gig. Stacking them can give you a high gain setting that would normally require a third pedal. The order of the pedals you are stacking will make a difference in how they sound when they are both on. Most players place the lower gain pedal first, but it is all personal preference.

 **Track 122**

Listen to Track 122 for a Rockett Archer into a MXR Timmy, first off, then Archer on, then both on.

Players will also combine these two ideas and stack drive pedals and a boost for solos. This is great when you need high gain and a volume boost for leads. Keep in mind that this will increase your noise level and can cause issues with feedback.

 **Track 123**

Listen to Track 123 for a Rockett Archer into a MXR Timmy, and then into a Xotic RC Booster, first off, then Archer on, then Archer and Timmy on, finally with all three on.

If you place the boost pedal before the overdrives, like in the diagram for signal flow #2, the boost will push the drives. This gives a different tone than the previous clip with the boost after the drives.

 **Track 124**

Listen to Track 124 for a Xotic RC Booster into a Rockett Archer, and then into a MXR Timmy; first off, then Archer on, then Archer and Timmy on, and finally with all three on.

(None of the controls on the amp or pedals were changed for the last three clips.)

Stacking a fuzz with an overdrive is another technique that can be very useful. Fuzz pedals sound amazing but can be too spitty and unruly sounding for many players. If you stack a fuzz pedal with a low gain overdrive pedal, like an Archer pedal, you can smooth out the tone of the fuzz pedal a little. This can help keep some of the overall tone and feel of the fuzz while taming it down some. It is recommended that you place the fuzz before the overdrive when doing this.

 **Track 125**

Listen to Track 125 for a Way Huge Swollen Pickle fuzz into a Rockett Archer, first off, then Swollen Pickle on, then Swollen Pickle and Archer on.

Way Huge Swollen Pickle.

Stacking Modulation

While stacking modulation pedals isn't as common as stacking drive pedals, it can be very useful. A very common example of this is using a chorus and a tremolo to simulate a rotating speaker.

Studio guitar players are well known for using chorus pedals to emulate the sound of a rotating speaker. This is often done by turning the depth up and setting the rate to the speed you need. The sound is close to that of a real rotating speaker, but it doesn't recreate the volume change of the speaker rotating. If you add a tremolo pedal after the chorus pedal and stack the two, you can achieve a sound that is closer to that of an actual rotating speaker. (Using the chorus without the tremolo is still a great way of faking a Leslie. The stacking of the two pedals just gives you another option.)

 **Track 126**

Listen to Track 126 for an Analogman Mini Chorus into a Strymon Flint set to "tremolo" to emulate a rotating speaker, first off and then both on.

The question often asked by players in response to this use of gear is, "Why?" Why would you use two pedals to get the sound that you can get with one pedal designed to emulate a rotating speaker?

1. The first reason to do this is if you don't own a pedal designed to only emulate a rotating speaker, but you do own a chorus and a tremolo. As hard as we try, most of us cannot own all the gear.

2. The second reason is due to pedalboard real estate. At some point most of us must stop adding pedals to our boards. We often run out of space, power, or both. So, if you need chorus and tremolo for multiple songs on your gig, but a rotating speaker sound on only one or two, you might need to make the sacrifice.

There are pedals that simulate a Leslie much more authentically than stacking a chorus and a tremolo. But sometimes we must sacrifice a little to make things work. Also, a sound that isn't a "perfect" recreation can work better for the part than the real thing.

Stacking Delays

Stacking delays is a very common technique used by guitarists. The Edge from U2 is well known for his masterful use of delays to create his sound, some of which are stacked. This technique is also very common in praise and worship music. Here are a couple common ways to stack delays.

Stacking Delays with Different Times

Some delay pedals allow the player to run two delays in parallel. This means that the two delays process the dry signal independently and do not stack. For example, if you set two delays in parallel, one set to a quarter note and the other to a dotted eighth note, you will hear the delays separately. The Strymon TimeLine is a great example of a delay that does this.

Many players stack two different delay times with two separate pedals or within one digital pedal. If you run two delays in series, the first delay will feed into the second, causing the second delay to sound on top of the first delay. This is the most common way guitarists stack delays. The audio clips of stacking digital and analog delays are done with the delays in series unless noted.

 Track 127

Listen to Track 127 for a Strymon TimeLine set to a parallel delay and then a series delay. The first pass has the delay off, the second set to parallel, and the third set to series. (The only delay setting that is changed is switching from parallel to series.)

Parallel delays can be done a few other ways as well. One option is to run two amps, each with its own dedicated delay. Another is to run a stereo delay that allows parallel processing into two amps. You should pan each delay to its own amp to achieve the same effect as running two independent delays to both amps. Both setups do require two amps, making a delay that allows parallel processing to one amp an easier option for most of us. (You can run parallel delays to more than two amps if you so desire.)

Stacking Digital and Analog Delays

Stacking digital and analog delays is also very common. Most players doing this use a simple analog delay with a short slap-back setting and a digital with a longer tap tempo setting. When running a mono setup, this can be done two different ways.

This option runs an analog delay into a digital delay. This allows you to hear the analog delay before the digital one. Some players prefer this sound over the next option below.

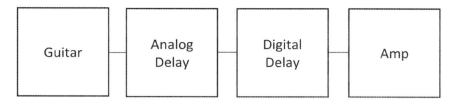

 **Track 128**

Listen to Track 128 for an Electro-Harmonix Deluxe Memory Man analog delay into a Strymon TimeLine digital delay, first off, then TimeLine on, then TimeLine and Memory Man on.

The second option runs a digital delay into an analog delay. This allows you to hear the analog delay after the digital one. While both work well, there is some psychological reasoning for using this particular option.

The recency and primacy effects on the brain show that we tend to remember the first and last things we hear more so than what is in the middle. This means that if we hear a note that has been delayed multiple times, we are more likely to remember the sound of the first and last notes more than the middle ones. If we apply this concept to stacking delays, the first note is our dry guitar signal and the last note is the last repeat of the analog delay. This leaves the warmth of the analog delay lingering in the listener's brain more than the digital delays. Again, there is not a right or wrong way of doing this. This is only a scientific reason why option two might sound better to your ears.

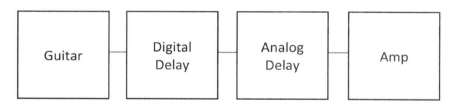

 **Track 129**

Listen to Track 129 for a Strymon TimeLine digital delay into an Electro-Harmonix Deluxe Memory Man analog delay, first off, then TimeLine on, then TimeLine and Memory Man on.

Gear used for recording:

Guitar: Les Paul, bridge pickup

Amp: 1972 Marshall Super Lead

Cabinet: Petersen 1x12, open-back

Speaker: Celestion Alnico Cream, 90-watt

Microphones: Shure SM57, Royer 121

CHAPTER 19

RIG OUTPUT OPTIONS

The output of your pedalboard to your amp or amps can be set up in multiple ways. The most common options are *mono*, *dual mono*, *stereo*, *wet/dry*, and *wet/dry/wet*. Here are some common ways to set up these rigs along with audio clips to hear the differences.

MONO

The most common rig used by guitarists is mono. This uses only one mono amp (some amps are stereo). This is usually done by coming out of your last pedal with a single guitar cable to the input of one amp (see diagram below). If your last pedal is a stereo pedal, you will use the output marked "mono." This is commonly the left output on a stereo pedal.

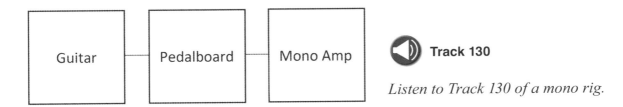

Track 130

Listen to Track 130 of a mono rig.

DUAL MONO

A dual mono rig uses two independent amps at the same time, but they do not have a stereo effect before them. This is often achieved by using a *splitter* or *ABY box* in the Y setting at the end of your pedalboard. (An ABY box is a pedal that allows you to send your signal to amp A or amp B, or to both amps simultaneously in the Y setting.) You can also come out of a stereo pedal and turn the effect off, causing the pedal to act as a splitter. This is often done with two different kinds of amps so that you get the tonal characteristics of both.

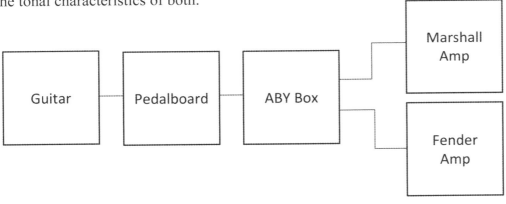

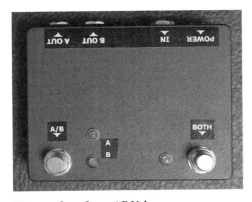

 **Track 131**

Listen to Track 131 of a dual mono rig with a Marshall amp on the left side and a Fender amp on the right.

Example of an ABY box.

STEREO

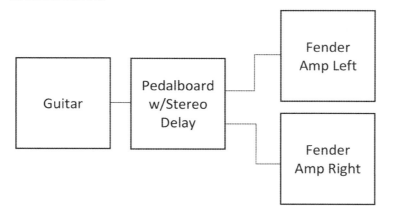

A stereo rig is most often one that uses two amps and has a stereo effect splitting the signal to both amps. (There are some amps, like the Roland JC120, that are stereo.) This is achieved by using a stereo effect at the end of your pedalboard. As stated in the previous section, if your stereo effect is turned off, your rig will technically be dual mono instead of stereo. Stereo rigs are more common than dual mono rigs because of how spacious stereo effects can sound. The audio clip for this example is done with a stereo ping-pong delay to emphasize the stereo spread. (I prefer using similar amps for a stereo rig, as opposed to different amps in a dual mono rig. This comes down to personal preference.)

 Track 132

Listen to Track 132 of a stereo rig with a Fender Vibrolux on the left side and a Fender '59 Bassman Reissue on the right side.

WET/DRY

A wet/dry rig splits the signal at the end of the drive section of your signal path. As with a standard dual mono rig, this is normally achieved by using a splitter or ABY box set to Y. The dry signal sent from the A side of the split does not have any modulation or time-based effects included. This is strictly the clean or overdriven tone. This dry signal goes to the first amp. The B side of the splitter box at the end of the drive section then goes into the modulation and time-based effects. This signal, with all of the drive section, modulation, and time-based effects, is then sent to a second amp. This design usually allows for more punch than a stereo rig due to the sound of the dry amp, but you lose some of the spaciousness created by a stereo rig. This is a dual mono rig, not a stereo rig. (Some players will send part of their modulation effects to the dry side. This is often due to how the pedals are being used.)

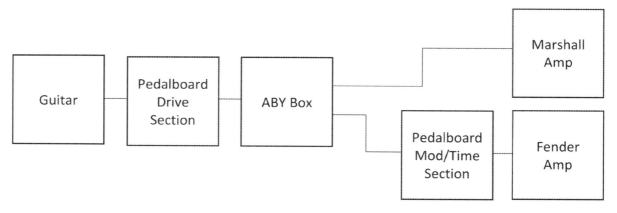

 Track 133

Listen to Track 133 of a dual mono rig with a dry Marshall amp on the left side and a wet Fender amp on the right.

WET/DRY/WET

A wet/dry/wet rig is laid out the same way, except that your wet signal is sent out stereo to two amps. The result of a wet/dry/wet rig can sound huge. The dry amp in the center helps maintain the punch of your tone, while the stereo effects allow for adding more space and depth to your overall sound. This is the most involved rig of all listed here, but it is also the most versatile.

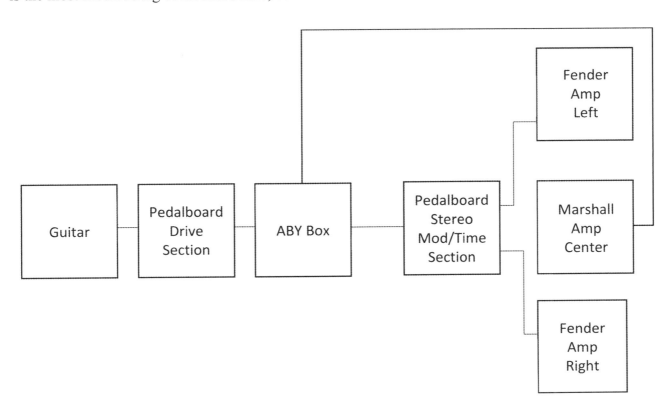

 **Track 134**

Listen to Track 134 for a wet/dry/wet rig. (The dry Marshall amp is in the center of the stereo field. The wet Fender amps are panned hard left and right with a ping pong stereo delay.)

Note: The wet and dry sections of the pedalboard do not have to be on separate boards. They are only represented this way to show the separation.

Gear used for recording:

Guitar: Les Paul, bridge humbucker

Amps: 1964 Fender Vibrolux Reverb, Fender '59 Bassman Reissue, 1972 Marshall Super Lead

Cabinet: Petersen 1x12, open-back (Marshall only)

Speaker: Tone Tubby Alnico Red 10" (Vibrolux), Weber 10A125 (Bassman), Celestion Alnico Cream, 90-watt (Marshall)

Microphone: SM57

CHAPTER 20
TROUBLESHOOTING YOUR RIG

No matter how well you take care of your rig, you will eventually have problems. Tubes wear out, solder connections break, batteries die, and somehow cables work their way out of the ins and outs they are connected to. While you might not be able to fix every problem that arises, here are a few troubleshooting tips that you might find helpful.

First and foremost, if your amp will not turn on with all the proper connections made, take it to a repair shop. The electrical current inside a guitar amp can be very high, even when it isn't connected to power. It is never a good idea to open one up and try to work on it if you are not qualified to do so. I highly recommend having a basic meter or cable tester to check cables and connections. This can make troubleshooting much easier and quicker. A small, battery-powered amp can also be very useful when checking cables. I will address ways to troubleshoot your rig without either.

NO SOUND WITH POWER

If you do not hear sound coming from your rig but everything is turned on, go through these steps to try and fix the issue.

1. First, check that the speaker cable is connected to your amp and your cabinet. Sending signal into a tube amp that is on but not connected to a speaker load can damage the amp. If you are using a combo, check the output from the amp and the connections to the speaker(s). Speaker connections, especially those that are clipped on instead of soldered, can work themselves loose. Change out the speaker cable, if possible, in case that cable has gone bad.

2. Check the cable from your guitar to your board by using it to plug your guitar straight into your amp. If that works, do the same with the cable that goes from your board to your amp. If they both work, then the issue is probably with your pedalboard. If only one works, you probably have a bad cable. Swap that cable for a good one and the issue should go away.

3. If you have an effects loop, check the connections to it. If you are using the loop, make sure that the connections are secure and plugged in correctly. It is very easy to reverse the send and return connections on a loop. Next, if you still do not have sound, disconnect the loop all together. If you are still not hearing anything, you probably need to take your amp to a repair shop.

4. If both cables mentioned in Step 2 do not pass signal, the issue is probably with your guitar or amp. While it is possible that both cables are bad, it is not probable. Take each one of the cables, plug them into the amp, and tap the ends. If only one cable makes noise, the issue is the other cable. If both do not make noise, the issue is probably with your amp (skip to Step 6). If both make noise, the issue is probably with your guitar (continue to Step 5).

5. If you discover that the guitar is the problem, there are only a couple things that are probably creating it. First, if you have an active guitar, replace the battery. Active pickups or an active preamp circuit normally require a standard 9-volt battery. A new battery will fix the issue if your current one is dead. (Keep in mind that batteries in guitars run whenever the output of the guitar is plugged in. So if you are done playing for a time, remember to unplug the guitar and save your battery life.)

   For those of us using passive guitars that do not have a battery, or if the battery swap didn't work, flip through all your pickups. You can lose just one of your pickups due to it dying or having a bad solder connection. If one pickup is bad, then this is the case. But if you still do not have signal, there is probably a bad connection within your guitar. The most common connections to go bad are the hot and ground connections at the output jack. This is an easy fix if you know how to use a soldering iron. Only do this type of work if you know how to safely use an iron. If not, off to the repair shop you go.

6. If the issue is with the amp, check to see if a tube has worked loose from its socket. If one is loose, cover your hand with a glove or rag and gently reinsert it into the correct socket. Never grab a hot tube without some type of covering on your hand. If this isn't the case and all the connections are made correctly with the amp and cab, the standby and power switches are both set to "on," and there isn't a mute button turned on (some amps do have mute buttons), then you probably need to take the amp to a repair shop.

7. If you discover the issue is with your pedalboard, start at the end of your pedalboard and plug into the pedals starting with the last one in your chain. If that works, then check the last two, then the last three, and so on. At some point, you will probably find a pedal that is causing a break in the signal. It is probably a bad cable and can be easily fixed with a replacement. If not, you could have a bad pedal.

8. If you are having power issues with your pedalboard, make sure that the connections to your power supply are secure. Second, try using a different IEC cable or wall wart-style power adapter, whatever your power supply of choice needs. Make sure you use the correct power adapter if your power supply requires one. Connecting the wrong power adapter can destroy your power supply. If this does not work, you will probably need to replace your power supply.

Sometimes you will lose power to one pedal when using an isolated power supply. This can be due to a single bad output, using the wrong output, or using the wrong power cable. Make sure you check your connections, swap cables if necessary, and check the manuals for your pedals and power supply to make sure you are making the correct connections. If some of the individual outputs on an isolated power supply are not working, those individual outputs are probably dead. You should take your power supply to a repair shop. If you are having power issues with a non-isolated power supply, you might not have enough power. Refer to Chapter 6 to reference how to deal with this.

NOISE ISSUES

Noise issues are also common problems with guitar rigs. They are normally broken down into four major categories.

Cables

Intermittent cables often cause a crackling noise in a rig. This is normally a very simple fix. You should check every cable from your guitar to your cabinet by gently shaking it. The bad cable should be obvious and easy to replace. You can hear an intermittent cable on Track 30. (Broken cables will stop any signal from passing.)

Digital Noise

Digital noise can be caused by a pedal not getting enough power. You will need to change the power supply for that pedal to fix the issue. You can hear this type of digital noise on Track 29.

Low Power

Lower power is often caused by one of two things. First, an intermittent cable can be the cause of your amp not sounding as loud as it should. If you use the techniques discussed earlier to troubleshoot your cables, you should be able to find the issue and easily fix it. Second, tubes that are going bad in a tube amp can also cause a drop in volume. The best thing to do for this issue is to take the amp to a reputable repair person.

Noisy Cable

It is easy to accidentally use a speaker cable in place of an instrument cable. This will cause an excessive amount of noise in your rig. If you hear this, make sure you are using the proper cables in the correct locations.

CHAPTER 21

MATCHING TONES TO STYLES

Music is categorized into different styles due primarily to the sound of the artist. While this can be easily recognizable with some artists, the blurring of the lines that used to separate styles is more present now than ever. This results in some wonderful music and creative guitar tones.

For example, a Telecaster into a clean Fender amp used to be known as the sound of country guitar. While it wasn't the only type of rig played in the genre, it was the primary one. Now you see country bands using all kinds of guitars and even some high gain amps for the modern country sound. Paul Reed Smith guitars now have a very strong presence in the Nashville country music scene, especially with touring players. Orange and Mesa Boogie amps are also seen on country tours and sessions every day. This doesn't mean that the music isn't country; it only means that the sound and gear associated with that style has changed.

Another great example of the development of tone and the use of gear is in the jazz world. Traditional jazz guitarists, such as Wes Montgomery, Charlie Christian, and Jim Hall were known for using archtops plugged directly into clean Fender amps or solid-state amps. (Polytone amps have always been a staple among jazz guitarists due to their clean tone and light weight.) Now modern jazz guitarists are using all types of effects, amps, and guitars to create new sounds. Pat Metheny, John McLaughlin, and Kurt Rosenwinkel are just a few examples of jazz guitarists who have developed unique sounds outside of the traditional clean jazz guitar tone. Even the late, great Jim Hall used a Digitech Whammy pedal towards the end of his life to create new sounds.

The use of extended range instruments such as 7-, 8-, and 9-string guitars are generally associated with modern metal and shredder guitar players. Steve Vai's album *Passion and Warfare*, along with the music of bands like Korn, helped solidify the use of these instruments within the genres. But the 7-string guitar was originally introduced into western music in the 1930s by jazz great George Van Eps. The use of 7-string guitars was primarily associated with jazz for decades before it was introduced in the shredder and metal community.

The beauty of all this is that the hard and fast rules of what gear you can and can't play within a style of music isn't nearly what it used to be. What is most important is what you play and the tone you use to play the music with. Since it would be nearly impossible to address all the gear used in every style of music, let's look at the more traditional sounds. This will help you know where to start and allow you to develop your own rig and tones. Remember, there are exceptions to every rule when it comes to tone. The information presented here is designed to help you understand what is commonly used today within these styles. What you develop for your own tone is completely up to you.

ROCK

The term *rock guitar* encompasses an enormous amount of music, as do the tones associated with the music. Rock guitarists have used every possible type of guitar, amp, and effect at one point or another to achieve their desired sound.

One tone that is strongly associated with rock guitar is that of a Les Paul into a Marshall. This sound is still regarded as one of the "holy grail" tones. Once you add in a handful of effects, you have a tried-and-true rig for rock guitar. Effects such as fuzz, wah, overdrive, phase, chorus, delay, and reverb are often used in rock guitar rigs. Here is a common layout for a versatile rock guitar rig:

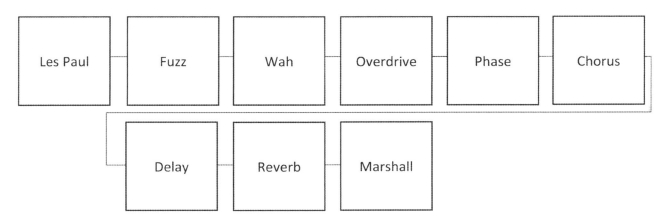

 **Track 135**

Listen to Track 135 for a rock guitar tone.

POP

As with rock, the genre of pop includes a large amount of music and guitar tones. The Beatles, Prince, Michael Jackson, Miley Cyrus, Taylor Swift, David Bowie, and Billy Joel are just a few examples of pop music artists that show the vastness of the genre. Considering how much music is classified under the umbrella of pop, let's look at some of the common aspects of their guitar tones.

Pop guitarists almost always begin with a great clean tone. Stratocaster-style guitars into Fender- or Vox-style amps are a great place to start for this. The use of effects such as compression, overdrive, chorus, tremolo, delay, and reverb are very common to build on top of the clean amp. Here is a common rig for pop guitar:

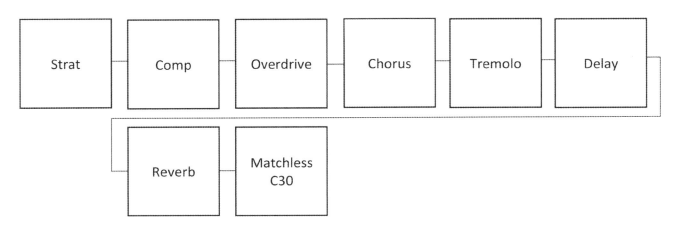

Matchless HC30 amplifier.

 **Track 136**

Listen to Track 136 for a pop guitar tone.

TRADITIONAL COUNTRY

Traditional country music artists like Johnny Cash, Waylon Jennings, Willie Nelson, and Dolly Parton helped define the sound of the genre. Today, artists such as Brad Paisley, Keith Urban, Brothers Osborne, and Chris Stapleton have expanded on the tradition while keeping the roots present. As with all genres of music, guitar players are known to use anything and everything. But there are a few staples we should observe.

Traditional country players, and those influenced by the tradition, normally use a Telecaster-style guitar into a Fender-style amp for the signature, twangy sound. The late, great Chet Atkins played a Gretsch for a large part of his career, as does Steve Wariner when he isn't playing one of his Strats. Brad Paisley is well known for using Vox-style amps, while Keith Urban has been known to use just about every amp imaginable at one point or another. But they still get the country sound they are famous for.

The quickest way to achieve the country twang is to start with a Tele, a Fender amp, and a handful of pedals. A compressor, overdrive, boost, volume pedal, vibrato, and delay are a great place to start. Since many Fender amps have reverb and tremolo built in, let's lay out the rig with that in mind.

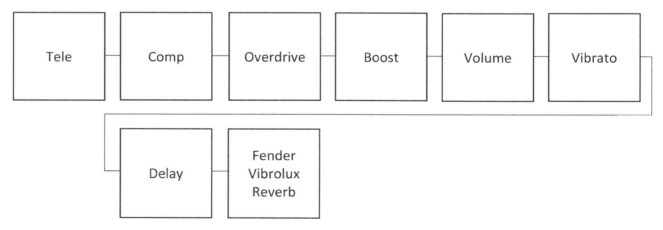

 **Track 137**

Listen to Track 137 for a traditional country guitar tone.

MODERN COUNTRY

The term *modern country* often refers to artists who have a sound that is heavily influenced by other styles of music, especially rock and rap.

Modern country artists like Brantley Gilbert, Colt Ford, and Jason Aldean are only a few who have blurred the lines between traditional country music, rock, metal, and rap. The use of heavy guitar tones and drop tuning show the influence of other genres of music in the modern country style. Depending on the artists, this can be more prominent on the stage than in the studio.

Modern country guitar tones are often achieved with Paul Reed Smith guitars, higher-gain amps, and a handful of effects. A normal rig for these players would include a compressor, two overdrives, a boost, volume, chorus, tremolo, delay, and reverb. Every type of amp imaginable can be seen on stage with these artists. The audio clip here is done with a Naylor Superdrive 60. These amps are somewhat rare, but they're still popular among pros. Studio great Chris Leuzinger is known for using the same amp while touring with Garth Brooks.

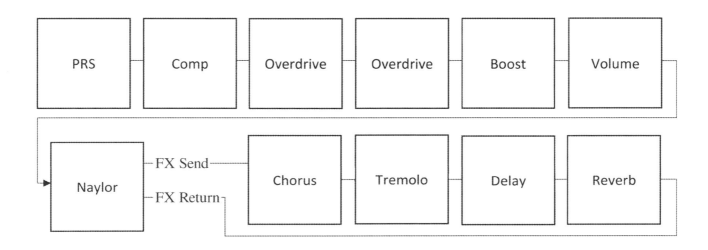

Naylor SD60 amplifier.

 **Track 138**

Listen to Track 138 for a modern country guitar tone.

JAZZ

Traditional jazz guitar tones are most often achieved by plugging a hollow body or archtop guitar into a clean sounding Fender-style or solid-state amp. The only effect that is often used for this sound is reverb. This results in a very simple rig used to create very complex music. Here is an example of a Redentore archtop guitar plugged into a solid-state Acoustic Image amp with a Raezer's Edge 1x12 Cabinet.

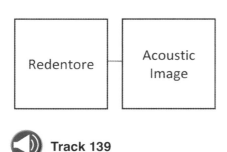

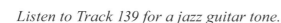

Track 139

Listen to Track 139 for a jazz guitar tone.

Acoustic Image amplifier head and Raezer's Edge cabinet, single 12" speaker.

METAL

Metal, as with every other genre of music, has multiple sub-genres. But one thing that stays common throughout them all is a heavily distorted, big guitar tone. The wall of distorted guitar is one of the defining elements of the style.

Classic metal relied heavily on modified Marshall amps in the '70s and '80s. The introduction of companies like Mesa Boogie, Friedman, Fryette, Bogner, and Soldano helped refine that sound with their own take on high-gain amps.

Today, while a lot of metal guitarists still use amps, many of them use modelers to achieve their tone. Both are valid rigs and can sound amazing. One thing that modelers do have that classic tube amps do not is the ability to process a wider sonic spectrum within the 20hz to 20k range. This gives modelers an advantage when using extended range instruments, synth-type effects, and pitch-shifting effects.

Here is a common setup for a metal tone within a Line 6 HX Stomp XL. The guitar used is a Forshage Guitars Orion 7-string tuned to drop A for the extended bottom end.

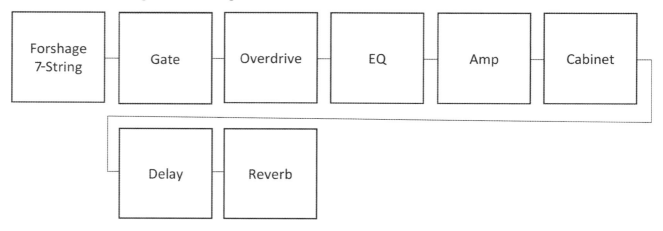

Forshage Orion.

 Track 140

Listen to Track 140 for a metal guitar tone.

FUNK

Funk guitar tones can go from clean to overdriven to all-out fuzz. The guitar players for James Brown, Michael Jackson, George Clinton, and Bruno Mars all have one thing in common: groove. While the parts played by these musicians often sound easy, playing them correctly can be another story. They are notorious for playing parts that build up a song like a section in an orchestra.

The tones they get are similar in that they focus on working for the music. They often just fit in the song just like the parts being played. These tones don't always stand out, but you would really miss them if they weren't there.

Funk guitarists often play Stratocaster or semi-hollow style guitars into clean Fender amps. The most common effects are going to be fuzz, wah, compression, overdrive, delay, and reverb.

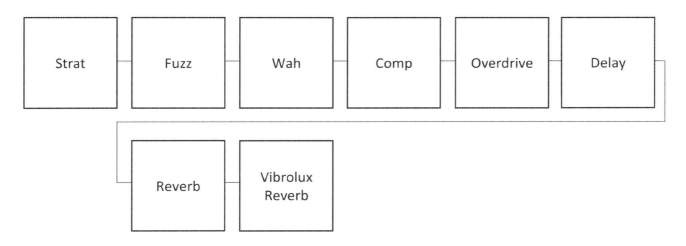

 **Track 141**

Listen to Track 141 for a funk guitar tone.

BLUES

The blues is a style of music that has influenced almost every genre of popular music out there. It can be heard in rock, country, metal, jazz, pop, and funk, to name a few. Just like the versatility of the music, the sound of the guitarists who play that music varies greatly.

The most popular guitars in blues are the Stratocaster, semi-hollow, and Les Paul-style guitars. But you can also see Flying Vs (Albert King), Telecasters (Albert Collins), and Explorers (Gary Moore), to name a few other popular options.

The amps are often Fender- or Marshall-style amplifiers, but also range from B.B. King's solid-state Gibson Lab Series to Joe Bonamassa's Dumble. The sound has changed dramatically since the recordings of Robert Johnson and his acoustic guitar.

The truth about blues guitar and gear is that there aren't any limits. Slide great Derek Trucks plugs his guitar straight into a Fender-style amp for his tone, while shredder Joe Satriani, who definitely has his style rooted in the blues, plays his signature model Ibanez guitar into a multitude of effects and high-gain amplifiers. (No, Satriani is not considered a blues player, but the influence of the music cannot be denied in his playing.)

With all these options, let's look at a rig that most blues guitarists would be happy to play.

A standard rig would be either a Les Paul or a Strat, fuzz, wah, a compressor primarily used for slide, overdrive, a rotary pedal, delay, and reverb.

 **Track 142**

Listen to Track 142 for a blues guitar tone.

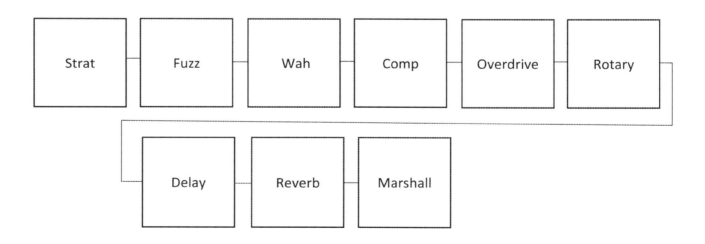

Gear used for recording:

All gear is listed by clip.

Microphones: Shure SM57, Royer 121

MAJOR RECORDINGS USING THE GEAR WE HAVE DISCUSSED

Stratocaster Style

Stevie Ray Vaughan and Double Trouble, "Pride and Joy"

Jimi Hendrix, "The Wind Cries Mary"

Jeff Beck, "Guitar Shop"

Yngwie Malmsteen, "Rising Force"

Telecaster Style

Brad Paisley, "Me Neither"

ZZ Top, "Jesus Just Left Chicago"

Rage Against the Machine, "Killing in the Name"

Mike Stern, "Upside Downside"

Les Paul Style

Tool, "Sober"

The Allman Brothers, "Ramblin' Man"

Guns N' Roses, "Sweet Child O' Mine"

Ozzy Osbourne, "Miracle Man"

Les Paul with P-90s

Mountain, "Mississippi Queen"

Green Day, "American Idiot" (live)

Pink Floyd, "Another Brick in the Wall, Pt. 2" (solo)

Carl Perkins, "Blue Suede Shoes"

335 Style (Semi-Hollow)

Steely Dan, "Kid Charlemagne" (solo)

Cream, "Badge"

Rush, "Anthem"

Eric Johnson, "Cliffs of Dover"

Paul Reed Smith Style

Shinedown, "Bully"

John Mayer, "Last Train Home"

Orianthi, "How Do You Sleep"

Periphery, "Graveless"

Archtop

Peter Bernstein, "Little Green Men"

Jim Hall, "My Funny Valentine"

Pat Metheny, "Bright Size Life"

Yes, "Leave Well Alone" (solo)

Baritone

Dave Matthews Band, "The Space Between"

Staind, "Mudshovel"

Brad Paisley, "I'm Still a Guy"

Josh Turner, "Would You Go with Me"

12-String

Led Zeppelin, "Stairway to Heaven"

The Eagles, "Hotel California"

The Byrds, "Eight Miles High"

The Beatles, "Ticket to Ride"

Active Pickups

Ozzy Osbourne, "Miracle Man"

Slipknot, "Duality"

Toto, "Falling in Between" (live)

Metallica, "Enter Sandman"

Fender-Style Amp

Brian Setzer, "Rock This Town"

Nirvana, "Lithium"

Dick Dale, "Miserlou"

Derek & The Dominos, "Layla"

Marshall-Style Amp

Jimi Hendrix, "Machine Gun" (live)

Guns N' Roses, "Welcome to the Jungle"

Van Halen, "Runnin' with the Devil"

Rage Against the Machine, "Bulls on Parade"

Vox-Style Amp

Brad Paisley, "Make a Mistake"

The Beatles, "Rain"

Queen, "Bohemian Rhapsody"

U2, "With or Without You"

Solid-State Amps

King's X, "Over My Head"

Pantera, "Cowboys from Hell"

The Police, "Every Breath You Take"

George Benson, "This Masquerade"

Overdrive

Stevie Ray Vaughan & Double Trouble, "Couldn't Stand the Weather"

AC/DC, "You Shook Me All Night Long"

Joe Bonamassa, "Time Clocks"

Gov't Mule, "Thorazine Shuffle"

Distortion

Foo Fighters, "I'll Stick Around"

Metallica, "Seek & Destroy"

R.E.M., "What's the Frequency, Kenneth?"

Joe Satriani, "I Believe" (solo)

Fuzz

The White Stripes, "Seven Nation Army"

The Rolling Stones, "(I Can't Get No) Satisfaction"

Lenny Kravitz, "Are You Gonna Go My Way"

Jimi Hendrix, "Purple Haze"

Octavia

Jimi Hendrix, "Who Knows" (live, solo)

Jimi Hendrix, "Purple Haze"

Kenny Wayne Shepherd Band, "Blue on Black"

Them Crooked Vultures, "Scumbag Blues"

Compression

Brad Paisley, "She's Everything"

Little Feat, "Dixie Chicken"

Steely Dan, "Peg" (solo)

Toto, "99" (outro solo)

Chorus

The Police, "Message in a Bottle"

Alice in Chains, "Rooster"

Nirvana, "Smells Like Teen Spirit"

Metallica, "Welcome Home (Sanitarium)"

Tremolo

The Rolling Stones, "Gimme Shelter"

Bruce Springsteen, "Born to Run"

Green Day, "Boulevard of Broken Dreams"

The Black Keys, "Howlin' for You"

Vibrato

Brad Paisley, "Little Moments"

Desert Rose Band, "He's Back and I'm Blue"

Blur, "Tender"

The Beatles, "It's Only Love"

Phase

Van Halen, "Eruption"

Van Halen, "Mean Street" (bridge)

Waylon Jennings, "Are You Sure Hank Done It This Way"

Smashing Pumpkins, "Mayonaise"

Flange

Van Halen, "Unchained"

Van Halen, "Ain't Talkin' 'Bout Love"

Heart, "Barracuda"

Rush, "The Spirit of Radio"

Uni-Vibe

Jimi Hendrix, "Machine Gun" (live)

Kenny Wayne Shepherd Band, "Blue on Black"

Pearl Jam, "Alive" (solo)

Pink Floyd, "Breathe (In the Air)"

Rotary

Stevie Ray Vaughan and Double Trouble, "Cold Shot"

Gov't Mule, "Thorazine Shuffle"

Mastodon, "Joseph Merrick"

The Rolling Stones, "Let It Loose"

Wah

Jimi Hendrix, "Voodoo Child (Slight Return)"

Metallica, "Enter Sandman" (Solo)

Joe Satriani, "Summer Song"

Rage Against the Machine, "Bulls on Parade"

Envelope Filter

John Mayer, "Wildfire" (solo)

U2, "Mysterious Ways"

Edie Brickell & New Bohemians, "What I Am" (solo)

Grateful Dead, "Shakedown Street"

Talk Box

Peter Frampton, "Do You Feel Like I Do"

Motley Crüe, "Kickstart My Heart" (solo)

Aerosmith, "Sweet Emotion"

Joe Walsh, "Rocky Mountain Way"

Pitch Shift

Allan Holdsworth, "Metal Fatigue"

Steve Vai, "Ballerina 12/24"

The White Stripes, "Seven Nation Army" (bass line is a guitar with an octave pedal)

Led Zeppelin, "Fool in the Rain" (solo)

Pitch Shift with Expression Control

Audioslave, "Like a Stone" (solo)

Joe Satriani, "Searching"

The White Stripes, "Seven Nation Army" (solo)

Pantera, "Becoming"

Ring Modulation

Black Sabbath, "Paranoid" (solo)

Prince, "Rainbow Children"

The Flaming Lips, "They Puncture My Yolk"

Wayne Krantz, "beLls"

Delay

Pink Floyd, "Run Like Hell"

U2, "Where the Streets Have No Name"

Guns N' Roses, "Welcome to the Jungle"

Dream Theater, "Pull Me Under"

Reverb

Dick Dale, "Miserlou"

Led Zeppelin, "When the Levee Breaks"

Eric Johnson, "Cliffs of Dover"

Pink Floyd, "Shine on You Crazy Diamond"

Synth/Oddball Effects

David Bowie, "Little Wonder"

John Scofield & Pat Metheny, "The Red One" (Pat Metheny part)

Muse, "Supermassive Black Hole"

Red Hot Chili Peppers, "Savior" (solo)

ACKNOWLEDGMENTS

Thank you to the following people for all their help with this project. It would not have been possible without them.

My incredible wife Kassandra Green, my loving parents for their support, my mentor Shane Roberts, Dave "Rock Star" Graef, Blair White, and Brandon Blane and their staff at Eastside Music Supply, the staff at Corner Music, Joey O. and Mitch Bennett with Dunlop/MXR/Way Huge, Scott Appleton, Trace Davis at Voodoo Amps, Reid Dern, Josh Cross, Nick Watkins, Analogman Mike Piera, Justin Butler at Thru-Tone FX and Modifications, John Pell and Paulo Oliveira with Belmont University, Chris Forshage at Forshage Custom Instruments, Chad Weaver, Chip Henderson, Mike Valeras, Bryan Clark, Ryan Wariner, Cedarstone School of Music, Jen Allen, Alex Stegall, Steve Uncapher at Gibson Guitars, Zac Childs, and TA and CJ from Weber Speakers.

ABOUT THE AUTHOR

Stephen Davis has been playing 6- and 7-string guitar since the late 1980s. He has a bachelor's degree in Commercial Music from Belmont University's School of Music, where he has been an adjunct faculty member since 2012. His work as a guitarist, instructor, technician, audio engineer, and composer has taken him all over the world. He currently resides in Nashville, Tennessee with his wife Kassandra and his Yorkies Rascal, Penny, and Smoky. You can contact him on his website, **www.stephendavismusic.com**.

play like
The Ultimate Lesson

Study the trademark songs, tones, and techniques of your heroes with this book/audio series. The comprehensive books provide detailed analysis of legendary artists' styles, songs, licks, riffs, and much more. Audio examples available online for download or streaming provide valuable demonstration assistance. And each book includes actual music examples and full song transcriptions to solidify your lessons!

GUITAR

PLAY LIKE CHET ATKINS
00121952 Book/Online Audio $24.99

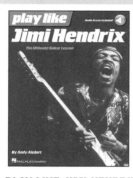

PLAY LIKE JIMI HENDRIX
00127586 Book/Online Audio $29.99

PLAY LIKE METALLICA
00248911 Book/Online Audio $24.99

BASS

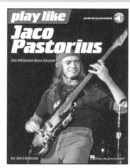

PLAY LIKE JACO PASTORIUS
00128409 Book/Online Audio $24.99

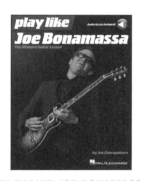

PLAY LIKE JOE BONAMASSA
00295491 Book/Online Audio $29.99

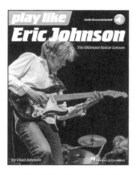

PLAY LIKE ERIC JOHNSON
00139185 Book/Online Audio $26.99

PLAY LIKE JOE PASS
00141819 Book/Online Audio $29.99

DRUMS

PLAY LIKE KEITH MOON
00148086 Book/Online Audio $19.99

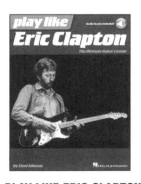

PLAY LIKE ERIC CLAPTON
00121953 Book/Online Audio $24.99

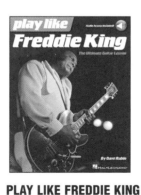

PLAY LIKE FREDDIE KING
00122432 Book/Online Audio $27.99

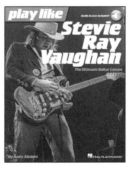

PLAY LIKE STEVIE RAY VAUGHAN
00127587 Book/Online Audio $27.99

PIANO

PLAY LIKE ELTON JOHN
00128279 Book/Online Audio $19.99

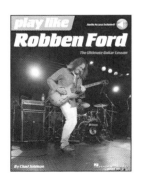

PLAY LIKE ROBBEN FORD
00124985 Book/Online Audio $22.99

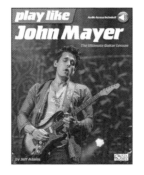

PLAY LIKE JOHN MAYER
00144296 Book/Online Audio $19.99

PLAY LIKE T-BONE WALKER
00255175 Book/Online Audio $19.99

HAL•LEONARD®
www.halleonard.com
Visit our website to see full song lists.

Prices, content, and availability subject to change without notice.

0323
313

Get Better at Guitar

...with these Great Guitar Instruction Books from Hal Leonard!

101 GUITAR TIPS
STUFF ALL THE PROS KNOW AND USE
by Adam St. James
This book contains invaluable guidance on everything from scales and music theory to truss rod adjustments, proper recording studio set-ups, and much more.
00695737 Book/Online Audio $17.99

AMAZING PHRASING
by Tom Kolb
This book/audio pack explores all the main components necessary for crafting well-balanced rhythmic and melodic phrases. It also explains how these phrases are put together to form cohesive solos. The companion audio contains 89 demo tracks, most with full-band backing.
00695583 Book/Online Audio $22.99

ARPEGGIOS FOR THE MODERN GUITARIST
by Tom Kolb
Using this no-nonsense book with online audio, guitarists will learn to apply and execute all types of arpeggio forms using a variety of techniques, including alternate picking, sweep picking, tapping, string skipping, and legato.
00695862 Book/Online Audio $22.99

BLUES YOU CAN USE
by John Ganapes
This comprehensive source for learning blues guitar is designed to develop both your lead and rhythm playing. Includes: 21 complete solos • blues chords, progressions and riffs • turnarounds • movable scales and soloing techniques • string bending • utilizing the entire fingerboard • and more.
00142420 Book/Online Media...............................$22.99

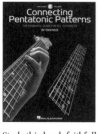

CONNECTING PENTATONIC PATTERNS
by Tom Kolb
If you've been finding yourself trapped in the pentatonic box, this book is for you! This hands-on book with online audio offers examples for guitar players of all levels, from beginner to advanced. Study this book faithfully, and soon you'll be soloing all over the neck with the greatest of ease.
00696445 Book/Online Audio $24.99

FRETBOARD MASTERY
by Troy Stetina
Untangle the mysterious regions of the guitar fretboard and unlock your potential. This book familiarizes you with all the shapes you need to know by applying them in real musical examples, thereby reinforcing and reaffirming your newfound knowledge.
00695331 Book/Online Audio $22.99

GUITAR AEROBICS
by Troy Nelson
Here is a daily dose of guitar "vitamins" to keep your chops fine tuned! Musical styles include rock, blues, jazz, metal, country, and funk. Techniques taught include alternate picking, arpeggios, sweep picking, string skipping, legato, string bending, and rhythm guitar.
00695946 Book/Online Audio $24.99

GUITAR CLUES
OPERATION PENTATONIC
by Greg Koch
Whether you're new to improvising or have been doing it for a while, this book/audio pack will provide loads of delicious licks and tricks that you can use right away, from volume swells and chicken pickin' to intervallic and chordal ideas.
00695827 Book/Online Audio $24.99

PAT METHENY – GUITAR ETUDES
Over the years, in many master classes and workshops around the world, Pat has demonstrated the kind of daily workout he puts himself through. This book includes a collection of 14 guitar etudes he created to help you limber up, improve picking technique and build finger independence.
00696587...$17.99

PICTURE CHORD ENCYCLOPEDIA
This comprehensive guitar chord resource for all playing styles and levels features five voicings of 44 chord qualities for all twelve keys – 2,640 chords in all! For each, there is a clearly illustrated chord frame, as well as *an actual photo* of the chord being played!.
00695224...$22.99

RHYTHM GUITAR 365
by Troy Nelson
This book provides 365 exercises – one for every day of the year! – to keep your rhythm chops fine tuned. Topics covered include: chord theory; the fundamentals of rhythm; fingerpicking; strum patterns; diatonic and non-diatonic progressions; triads; major and minor keys; and more.
00103627 Book/Online Audio $27.99

SCALE CHORD RELATIONSHIPS
by Michael Mueller & Jeff Schroedl
This book/audio pack explains how to: recognize keys • analyze chord progressions • use the modes • play over nondiatonic harmony • use harmonic and melodic minor scales • use symmetrical scales • incorporate exotic scales • and much more!
00695563 Book/Online Audio $17.99

SPEED MECHANICS FOR LEAD GUITAR
by Troy Stetina
Take your playing to the stratosphere with this advanced lead book which will help you develop speed and precision in today's explosive playing styles. Learn the fastest ways to achieve speed and control, secrets to make your practice time really count, and how to open your ears and make your musical ideas more solid and tangible.
00699323 Book/Online Audio $22.99

TOTAL ROCK GUITAR
by Troy Stetina
This comprehensive source for learning rock guitar is designed to develop both lead and rhythm playing. It covers: getting a tone that rocks • open chords, power chords and barre chords • riffs, scales and licks • string bending, strumming, and harmonics • and more.
00695246 Book/Online Audio $22.99

Guitar World Presents STEVE VAI'S GUITAR WORKOUT
In this book, Steve Vai reveals his path to virtuoso enlightenment with two challenging guitar workouts – one 10-hour and one 30-hour – which include scale and chord exercises, ear training, sight-reading, music theory, and much more.
00119643...$16.99

HAL•LEONARD®

Order these and more publications from your favorite music retailer at
halleonard.com

Prices, contents, and availability subject to change without notice.